SPORTS FOR LIFE

Daily Sports Themes For Life Success

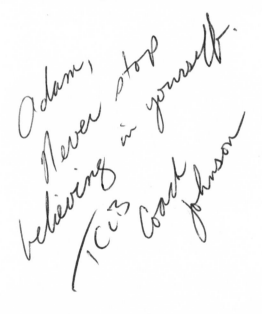

Adam,
Never stop
believing in yourself.
TCi's Coach Johnson

SPORTS FOR LIFE

Daily Sports Themes For Life Success

Sean T. Adams

Aventine Press

Published by Aventine Press
1023 4th Ave #204
San Diego CA, 92101
www.aventinepress.com

ISBN: 1-59330-379-3

Printed in the United States of America

For Pops,
rest in peace.
For mom,
who has never rested.

Contents

Introduction

I would like to think that this book; this compilation of narratives and quotes is for all people who love sports. For the athlete and the people that cheer them on to victory, these quotes of motivation, education, reality and perspective should lend an addition to the mindset of the competitor and wonderful group of supporters who, sometimes without knowing, are the purveyor of the pressure.

I can point to three things, other than achieving a personal level of success, which directed me to a love of sports, knowledge of sports and finally, a life in sports.

Family Influence

My father was an All-Everything high school baseball player and though a poor decision on his part derailed a potential pro career, his intensity, work ethic, and knowledge of the game and competition brought my family into the world of sports. His work with my brother and later with me, taught me about the value of not only working hard but also working smart.

"The Play"

November 20, 1982 was the day that really lit my candle about sports and particularly college football. My father, a bus driver for the county transit system, would sometimes score tickets to Oakland A's games, San Francisco Giants games, Golden State

Warrior games and on this occasion tickets to the Cal vs. Stanford game at Memorial Stadium.

I was blessed enough to be in the stands and see the five laterals, ending with Kevin Moen's destruction of Stanford trombone player, Gary Tyrrell, to score the winning touchdown and end the season of John Elway and the Stanford Cardinal.

ESPN

I, not unlike many people in this country, had a life changing experience on September 7, 1979 and didn't even know it at the time. I would view sports differently for the rest of my life as well as be encouraged and inspired. On that late summer day, Lee Leonard uttered these words…

"If you are a fan, what you'll see over the next minutes, hours and days to follow may convince you you've gone to sports heaven."

That was the first programming that Entertainment and Sports Programming Network aired and has now grown to and merged their way into the media monster called ESPN.

Media outlets like ESPN allowed me to saturate myself in sports and competition. Growing up during the cable television boom allowed me to see sports all day and in repetition.

Frustration is the main ingredient that aided in the development of this compilation of quotes. A number of athletes that I worked with for a couple years were graduating from high school and a few of them had been awarded football and/or track scholarships. I wanted to give them something that might encourage them as they started their college careers.

I visited or called nearly every bookstore in the Austin (TX) area trying to find something that might mirror my thoughts on the virtues, flaws and realities of sports and competition. I even took a pass at the Internet stores for something that would educate and inspire while relating enough, from a sports perspective, to hold their attention. A fairly good understanding of sports, athleticism and competition helped myself as well as many other athletes during their high school and college careers. I drew much of that understanding and perspective from my upbringing, my coaches and my teammates. After being reminded that "I always have a quote for everything"; I came up with the crazy idea to form a compilation myself.

And here it is...

Attitude

Attitude - a mental position with regard to a fact or state; a feeling or emotion toward a fact or state

I believe that everyone, on the surface, knows that for every "big-time" athlete who makes it to the top of their game, there are many others with equal talent who did not make it to the top. What is the characteristic that the talented individuals have that those who don't make it lack? Without regard to athletic talent, what is the most vital resource needed for an athlete to find success? Pat Hill, the Head Football Coach at Fresno State University, says that his team will play anyone, anywhere at anytime. He is trying to instill an attitude of toughness and selflessness in his program and it has worked. When you talk of attitude, it is a very broad spectrum because everyone doesn't have all the characteristics of attitude. There are different characteristics that must be possessed because situations vary and reality is different for everyone.

Against All Odds

The old credo that all men (and women) are created equal is just not true. Everyone starts with a different level of gifts, talents and abilities. Your attitude, not your aptitude, will determine your altitude. How high can your attitude take you is the question that you must answer.

Mike Edwards was born without a right fibula. Because that bone was missing it caused his leg to grow abnormally. He finally made the choice to have it amputated at 13 and learned to be mobile on a prosthetic. He loved the game of basketball. He actually made his high school team and played without his teammates knowing his condition. He wore sweat pants and though people thought it was weird, he did not have to tell his story until he decided the time was right. As it happened, the time was right on the team bus. He showed and then removed his prosthetic leg to the surprise of his high school teammates.

Because Mike's attitude was so good about not letting this one physical issue hold him back, he was able to walk-on to the team at the University of Notre Dame. His father had been stationed there while in the military and Mike fell in love with the Fighting Irish. He tried out for the Notre Dame Basketball team and made it. Mike Edwards smiled into a camera one day and said, "I don't have a leg and I'm playing Division I basketball."

Against seemingly all odds, Mike Edwards figured out how to fulfill his dream of playing basketball at Notre Dame.

Chuck

Chuck was a man that I used to work for. I referred to him as the messenger of misery. Most people in my group hated to work for him. He was often the subject of conversation at lunch and during meetings when he was not in attendance. It would not be seldom to hear, "Today sucks, I have to see Chuck," or "I'm happy, Chuck is out of town." When he was finally pushed out of the company, most people let out a silent or non-silent cheer. Someone even said to me, "We are going to lunch to celebrate, No More Chuck!" There will be a 'Chuck' around you all of your life. Chuck is constantly trying to deter you from your goals. Chuck could be a neighbor, an opposing coach, your coach, a teammate, the parent of a teammate or in simple terms, just a 'hater.' Chuck, especially when in a position of power, could have you troubled with anger and wondering how you can thrive, or even survive with him. In the words of American historian Roscoe Brown,

"You have to defuse your anger with humor, excellence or just plain arrogance."

Lance Armstrong met Chuck one day in the form of a cancer that started in his testicles and moved throughout his body. When testicular cancer is detected early, 9 out of 10 patients get cured. However, Lance Armstrong was no different than most young and healthy men, he ignored the warning signs. Because the condition went untreated, the cancer had time to spread to his abdomen, lungs and his brain. With that prognosis, his chances of survival looked really dim.

Lance Armstrong's special attitude took over when he declared himself not a cancer victim but a cancer survivor. As he learned and educated himself on his disease, he underwent aggressive treatment and that treatment, when coupled with his excellent physical condition and his confidence in his recovery program, allowed him to beat the disease.

He went on to win seven straight Tour De France road races from 1999 – 2005 and is widely acclaimed as the best cyclist in history.

The Moment

Before we actually get to the question about what you are thinking when the pressure is on, we have to ask the question, do you want to be there? Do you want to be counted on when the game is on the line? Do you show initiative when it's time for someone to step up and be the hero or do you shrink to the back of the line so you do not have to assume any responsibility or be relied on.

Your team is down by one, no time left on the clock, you are on the free-throw line, shooting two; what are you thinking?

One penalty kick to win the match and you are standing behind the ball. What are you thinking?

Bottom of the ninth, two outs and runners on second and third, down by one. Championship is on the line. What are you thinking?

You are on the 18th hole, down by one stroke with a 7 foot birdie putt to push a playoff. What are you thinking?

I would say that your attitude is more important than your skills when you are in the moment. When you are up against the pressure is when your attitude matters most. Your team, your coaches, your family and the fans are looking to you to make it happen. It is at that time that you have to embrace the moment, focus and be at your best in order to seize the opportunity.

Scott Bentley was the nation's best kicker during his senior year at Overland High School in Aurora, Colorado. When trying to make a choice for college, he came down to Notre Dame, which was coached by Lou Holtz and Florida State University, coached by Bobby Bowden. Considering the chronicled history of "wide-right" kicking woes for Florida State standing between them and a national championship, Bentley chose the Seminoles and headed south. To add a little more pressure to the shoulders of the young kicker, he made the cover of *Sports Illustrated* magazine and was hailed as the kicker that would be the final piece to bring the football national championship to Tallahassee.

A few short months into his freshman year, Bentley had the opportunity to be the kicker that everyone hoped he would be. In the Orange Bowl against Nebraska for the National Championship, the Seminoles found themselves down 15 – 14 with 21 seconds left in the game. Bentley later recalled, "This is what I was recruited for. I couldn't hide, the whole world was watching." Bentley stepped up and calmly knocked it through and won Coach Bobby Bowden his first National Championship.

It Ain't Gonna' Happen

One of the hardest things to face is the understanding that things are not going to pan out quite the way you planned. It does not matter how much you plan. It does not matter how much you try. Sometimes things just go the way of the other guy. I wanted to be a national champion in track and field. I had been a big contributor on a team national championship but had been relegated to second place many times in individual and relay events. Coming into my last meet as a senior, I was determined to win just one. After a freshmen, sophomore and junior year plagued by second place finishes, this was going to be the year. Though I qualified for the national meet in individual events and felt secure in making the finals, I knew that the relays were my best opportunity to win it all. We came into the meet listed among the top two or three teams in the 4 X 100 meter relay and the 4 X 400 meter relay. When the final in the 4 X 100 Relay was started, we were near the middle of the track. When it came to my leg of the race, the third leg, I went around that turn knowing that we were going to win. When I handed off for the anchor leg in first place, I raised my hands in the air, and realized I had finally been a part of an event national champion. As I jogged down the home-stretch hundred, I looked toward the finish line and saw the team in the lane next to mine raise their hands and start their celebratory trot. We got nipped at the tape. I had another second place finish. I could not get too low though, I still had other events to run.

When it came to the last event of the day, I was focused on my leg of the race. I was the anchor for the 4 X 400 meter relay. It was all on me and that is just the way I wanted it. 1st leg ran, then 2nd leg ran and then finally the 3rd leg made his run. As I see my teammate come down the homestretch, I was waving him in and I did my customary tuck jump before I get ready to go. I got the stick about five meters back but in solid second place. The guy in first place was a guy that I had run against before in the open 400 meters and other relay events. I focused on his back and in the middle of the back straight, I pulled up next to him. I still don't know why I didn't run past him like I was coached to do. If I had run past him, I could have made him run my race. Instead, I stayed right there with him and ran his race and in the pattern of running his race, he started pulling away from me with 40 meters to go and beat me and my team by the same five meter lead he started the leg with. In the process, I earned myself and my teammates another silver NCAA trophy for second place.

Lesson #1 – Do what your coaches tell you to do. They usually know more, and usually a lot more than you.

Lesson #2 – Understand your accomplishments, acknowledge your successes and give proper credence to your failures. At the end of the day, you have to learn from your successes and your failures. Giving yourself too much love for your successes is just as bad as giving yourself too much grief for your failures. Everything you experience is about learning, growing and moving forward. It would have been really nice to win a first place trophy at the NCAA national meet. Honestly, I still think about it from time to time. But, I readily acknowledge that the lessons I learned on the second level of the awards stand have helped me in life and given me perspective.

Sports on attitude...

"If not me: who? If not now, when? If not here, where?" - Lou Holtz

"Ain't no man can avoid being born average, but there ain't no man that gots to be common." - Satchel Paige

"The man who thinks he can and the man who thinks he can't are both right. Which one are you son, which one are you?" – High School Coach

"Anyone, any time, any place!" – Pat Hill

"Ability is what you're capable of doing. Motivation determines what you do. Attitude determines how well you do it." - Lou Holtz

"At that point, getting down on Florida State football was the most popular pastime in Florida, second only to getting down on Richard Nixon. But I believed differently. Eventually, so would everyone else." - Bobby Bowden

"With a positive attitude, it's so amazing what you can accomplish."
- Tyrone Willingham

"Do not let what you cannot do interfere with what you can do."
- John Wooden

"I don't believe you willing to give up the same thing that I'm willing to give up, just to win." – Ray Lewis

"To be great, you must be selfish. Period! You train with a selfish mentality. Game on the line – I'm making the play. If I train that way all the time; when I get in the game and those tough situations come up, I am all over the guys saying, 'Give me the ball, I trained for this.'" - Michael Irvin

"This cannot be a team of common men. Cause common men go nowhere. You have to be uncommon." - Herb Brooks

"Part of being a champ is acting like a champ. You have to learn how to win and not run away when you lose." - Nancy Kerrigan

"My thoughts before a big race are usually pretty simple. I tell myself: Get out of the blocks, run your race, stay relaxed. If you run your race, you'll win....Channel your energy. Focus!" - Carl Lewis

"Simply trying to define sportsmanship, I think most folks would agree responsibility and self respect, qualities that today seem in short supply at times. If character is what you do when no one is watching, then perhaps sportsmanship is that conduct with everybody watching? Frankly, the sports industry would probably survive without sportsmanship. It's so large and so well financed, but it would be refreshing if more parents and coaches, more administrators and more journalists, and especially more players realized there is room to win with flare and style and even get rich and still keep the values that first brought us here to the games." - Bob Ley

"Sports are a lot like photography. If you don't focus, all you will get is the negative." - Unknown

"You have no control over what the other guy does. You only have control over what you do." - A. J. Kitt

"It's my attitude, not my aptitude that will determine my altitude or how high I will go." - Unknown

"Do you know what my favorite part of the game is; the opportunity to play?" - Mike Singletary

"Nobody who ever gave his best regretted it." - George Halas

"A bad attitude is worse than a bad swing." - Payne Stewart

"Life's battles don't always go to the stronger or faster man. But sooner or later the man who wins, is the man who thinks he can." - Vince Lombardi

"Put it close." - Bruce Edwards

"Never let yesterday take up too much of today." - Texas E. Schramm

"In baseball you can never let losing carry over to the next day. You've got to flip the page." - Don Baylor

"Self discipline is an individual's greatest asset." - Lou Holtz

"I'm not the second coming of Greg Lemond, I'm the first coming of Lance Armstrong."
- Lance Armstrong

"You have to hear things you don't want to hear; you must look at things you really don't want to see." - John Madden

"Once you learn to quit, it becomes a habit." - Vince Lombardi

"Service to others is the rent you pay for your room here on earth."
- Muhammad Ali

"My father has always instilled in me there are only two things in life that you ought to do. You gotta' care and you gotta' share."
- Tiger Woods

"I'm gonna' have a good year and people are gonna' have to deal with it, whether they like me or not." - Chris Simms

"You can't just love the game because you're a great program; you win 11 games or you win 8 or 9 games. It doesn't work that way. The bottom line is, everyone can't win. I coached a football team that never won a game and every game I went on the field, I thought I could win." - Dennis Green

"For when the One Great Scorer comes to mark against your name, He writes not that you won or lost--but how you played the game!" - Grantland Rice

"While it's important to win, it's imperative to compete." - Dave Weinbaum

"When someone tells me there is only one way to do things, it always lights a fire under my butt. My instant reaction is, I'm gonna' prove you wrong." - Picabo Street

"When you have the attitude of a champion, you see adversity as your training partner." - Conor Gillen

"You have to defuse your anger with humor, excellence or just plain arrogance." - Roscoe Brown

Determination

Determination - direction or tendency to a certain end

When I was in high school, my cousin was an intern and working for the San Francisco 49ers as an Athletic Trainer. His relationship with our family got us access to not only games and the player parking lot but also the training camp at Sierra College in Rocklin, CA. My cousin always talked about the players, their habits and their personalities. After a few conversations with him about Joe Montana, I made it my business to find a way to meet him and listen to him.

I finally got my opportunity at a fishing event that the 49ers put together for the players, staff and their families. It was in a very confined space at a large fountain on the small college campus. I heard the stories about Joe Montana and his ability to compete, talk and laugh at the same time. He seemed to enjoy the game that he played. On this day I heard him competing and talking about which player would catch the first fish, the biggest fish, the most fish, etc. I was very impressed by him and made it a goal of mine to learn about him, his history and how he got to this place as quarterback of the world's best football team.

In short, I learned that he had to get there, as I would on a smaller scale later on with grit, fight and determination.

It took Joe Montana a long time to become who I think is the best quarterback in football history. To say he had some growing pains would be putting it mildly. While he was a very good high school quarterback, his first year on the varsity at Notre Dame in 1975, he found himself tenth on the quarterback depth chart. He did work himself up to second string during the pre-season, but didn't experience much success when he did get game time snaps. After getting snaps only because of injuries or low levels of team success, Joe Montana finally took over and led Notre Dame to the 1977 National Championship.

And the rest, as they say, is history…

- Four Superbowl Wins
- Three Superbowl Most Valuable Player Awards
- Three Time All NFL
- Five Time All NFC
- Eight Pro Bowls
- 2000 Enshrinement into the Pro Football Hall of Fame

I often thought about Joe Montana and where he was on the depth chart at Notre Dame in 1975 and the opposing sight I saw seven years later; when he completed "The Catch" to Dwight Clark in 1982 to beat the Dallas Cowboys and kick start a dynasty.

Sports on determination…

"There's no substitute for guts." - Paul "Bear" Bryant

"My motto was always to keep swinging. Whether I was in a slump or feeling badly or having trouble off the field, the only thing to do was keep swinging." - Hank Aaron

"You carry on no matter what the obstacles are. You simply refuse to give up - and, when the going gets tough, you get tougher. And, you win." - Vince Lombardi

"Everybody is looking for instant success, but it doesn't work that way. You build a successful life one day at a time." - Lou Holtz

"The difference between the impossible and the possible lies in a mans determination." - Tommy Lasorda

"It's a little like wrestling a gorilla. You don't quit when you're tired you quit when the gorilla is tired." - Robert Strauss

"When going through tough times, you either have to quit, you have to surrender or you have to fight back." - Lloyd Carr

"I've always made a total effort, even when the odds seemed entirely against me. I never quit trying; I never felt that I didn't have a chance to win." - Arnold Palmer

"The man who can drive himself further once the effort gets painful is the man who will win." - Sir Roger Bannister

"The only one who can tell you 'you can't' is you. And you don't have to listen." - Nike

"Don't give up, don't ever give up!" - Jim Valvano

"Motivation is what gets you started. Habit is what keeps you going." - Jim Ryun

"The trouble with some people is that during trying times they stop trying." - Unknown

"Gold medals aren't really made of gold. They're made of sweat, determination, and a hard-to-find alloy called guts." - Dan Gable

"If you get up one more time than you fall you will make it through." - Unknown

"Better to have died as a small boy than to fumble this football." - John Heisman

"Never quit. It is the easiest cop-out in the world. Set a goal and don't quit until you attain it. When you do attain it, set another goal, and don't quit until you reach it. Never quit." - Paul "Bear" Bryant

"People of mediocre ability sometimes achieve outstanding success because they don't know when to quit. Most men succeed because they are determined to." - George Allen

"Pain is temporary but glory is forever." - Unknown

"What makes you really come together under pressure is determination and focus and toughness." - Debi Thomas

Commitment

Commitment - the state or an instance of being obligated or emotionally impelled

Commitment is a word that many people know the dictionary meaning of but the fruition is where the disconnect takes place.

Most athletes and former athletes (me included) finally figure out the commitment that it takes to be successful to the extent of your potential after the whistle has blown for the last time. It is a sad state when you wake up one morning and your career is over. The career that I am talking about can be a high school, college or professional career. You take off that uniform for the last time. At some point shortly thereafter you discover that you left something on the table. You had a little left in the tank. You were leaving it on reserve for something. You never quite knew what that something was but you knew it was there. You were saving for a rainy day and you never deemed your situation as rainy.

That's the story that most athletes live with for the rest of their lives. Athletes do not feel the weight of the knowledge or the finality of the final game until it has come and gone. Hindsight brings them full circle and the gap between what was possible and what was given starts to build.

"25 years ago, everyone talked about their obligations and responsibilities, now everyone talks about their rights and their privileges. It all boils down to where your heart is." - **Lou Holtz**

Do you feel obligated to be the best you can be or are you satisfied with simply getting by?

Can your teammates, coaches and even in some regard the fans trust in you when it is crunch time?

Can you control yourself?

Can you do the small things to ensure that you will be there for your team?

As a student athlete, can you take care of business in the classroom to ensure that you take advantage of all of your opportunities?

Can you commit to preparation, practice and study?

Is your heart in your game, your job and your endeavor? Is that what you think about? Is that what "rents space" in your head. One of my favorite poker players is Phil Ivey and he has remarked on numerous occasions how his spending time in thought about the game of poker has made him a better player.

You cannot be great at any one thing without making a commitment to greatness. Many people talk about greatness but they are not able to truly commit to be the greatest that they can be.

Sports on commitment...

"The quality of a person's life is in direct proportion to their commitment to excellence, regardless of their chosen field of endeavor." - Vince Lombardi

"If you don't make a total commitment to whatever you're doing, then you start looking to bail out the first time the boat starts leaking. It's tough enough getting that boat to shore with everybody rowing, let alone when a guy stands up and starts putting his jacket on." - Lou Holtz

"Learn to do things right and then do them right every time." - Bobby Knight

"Rowing is a sport for dreamers. As long as you put in the work, you can own the dream. When the work stops, the dream disappears." - Jim Dietz

"Every game boils down to doing the things you do best and doing them over and over again." - Vince Lombardi

"Tiger Woods became Secretariat in the Belmont; so far ahead of the field that he clearly was a man playing on a higher course; a man in a zone that very few can understand and even fewer have attained." - Chris Berman

"If you aren't fired with enthusiasm, you'll be fired with enthusiasm."
- Vince Lombardi

"To give anything less than your best is to sacrifice the gift." – Steve Prefontaine

"Commitment to the team - there is no such thing as in-between, you are either in or out." - Pat Riley

"You never win a game unless you beat the guy in front of you. The score on the board doesn't mean a thing. That's for the fans. You've got to win the war with the man in front of you. You've got to get your man." - Vince Lombardi

"25 yrs. ago, everybody talked about their obligations and responsibilities. Today, everybody talks about their rights and their privileges." - Lou Holtz

"Talent is never enough. With a few exceptions, the best players are the hardest workers." - Ervin 'Magic' Johnson

"Not all heroes run on the field. Somebody has to clap as the heroes run by." - Jeremy Wells

Character

Character - one of the attributes or features that make up and distinguish an individual; the complex of mental and ethical traits marking and often individualizing a person, group, or nation

Because I have always considered my own athletic career to be derived from my definition of luck, timing, great coaching, a marginal amount of talent and a healthy naivety to what it took to be good, I have always enjoyed watching and learning the great stories of people whose character has lead them to victory.

That character, which manifests itself in so many different ways, means different things to different people.

While character could come into play in everything from workouts to practices to performance enhancers, character is not only shown in the physical activities of sports.

It comes back to playing "perfect" and by perfect, I'm not referring to the record at the end of a season or the score at the end of a competition. Perfect is the performance that everyone looks for. Perfect is the culmination of a season full of practices for one moment that could make a season. Perfect is having the character to play every second like it is your last. Perfect is a performance when finished leaves the competitor with no possible options they could have tried.

Do you have the character to give it your all? Do you have the character to look your teammates in the eyes at the end of a defeat and honestly say, "I gave everything I had in me to give. While not playing perfect, I did have perfect effort."

When you do win, is it with character? Were the books tilted in your favor? Did you cheat?

It all comes down to one question…

Who are you?

I'm not talking about what people think you are. To the people around you, you might be anything from the nice kid next door to a coach that cares about the kids.

When you are in your bed, by yourself; who are you?

When you have to make a choice between right and wrong and nobody is watching, who are you?

When something or someone is completely vulnerable to you, who are you?

Character, many times is one of our best motivators. Do you have the character to see a project that you have started through to its conclusion? Do you have the character to keep going even when those around you have given up, only because you made a commitment and are going to see it through? Do you have the character to keep practicing and playing hard when you are up against a winless season? Do you have the character to do your job even if you think there is a better way?

Character is one of the things that you have to allow yourself to be selfish about. It becomes all about you. Sometimes it is not good enough to be as good as the people around you. You have to compare yourself against what you are capable of as opposed to what others have done. That concept will keep you from settling for less.

At the end of the day, all you have is your character, and you have to protect it. Sometimes you have to protect it with blood, sweat and tears. At the end of it all, you can rest every night knowing you did the best you could with what you had and where you were right then.

Sports on character...

"It is essential to understand that battles are primarily won in the hearts of men." - Vince Lombardi

"There's no wrong way to do right and no right way to do wrong." – Joe Frazier

"Each Warrior wants to leave the mark of his will, his signature, on important acts he touches. This is not the voice of ego but of the human spirit, rising up and declaring that it has something to contribute to the solution of the hardest problems, no matter how vexing!" - Pat Riley

"The size of the battle should not create the heart of the champion." - Nick Saban

"Sports Do Not Build Character...They Reveal It" - John Wooden

"One player practicing sportsmanship is far better than 50 preaching it." - Knute Rockne

"The vision of a champion is someone who is bent over, drenched in sweat, at the point of exhaustion when no one else is watching."
- Anson Dorrance

"Champions aren't made in gyms. Champions are made from something they have deep inside them: A desire, a dream, a vision. They have to have late minute stamina, they have to be a little faster, and they have to have the skill and the will. But the will must be stronger than the skill." - Muhammad Ali

"Never give up, never give in, and when the upper hand is ours, may we have the ability to handle the win with the dignity that we absorbed the loss." - Doug Williams

"I always thought there was at least one person in the stands who had never seen me play, and I didn't want to let him down." - Joe Dimaggio

"But it's not about the names in the lineup. It's all about heart."
- Augie Garrido

"Be more concerned with your character than your reputation, because your character is what you really are; your reputation is merely what others think you are." - John Wooden

"Fame is a vapor, popularity is an accident, money takes wings, those who cheer you today may curse you tomorrow. The only thing that endures is character." - Horace Greeley

"The future belongs to those who see possibilities before they become obvious." - Unknown

"Doing what is right, fair, and honorable is more important than winning or losing." - Chick Moorman

"Loyalty is very important when things get a little tough, as they often do when the challenge is great. Loyalty is a powerful force in producing one's individual best and more so in producing a team's best." - John Wooden

"Every job is a self-portrait of the person who does it. Autograph your work with excellence." - Unknown

"If you're lucky enough to find a guy with a lot of head and a lot of heart, he's never going to come off the field second." - Vince Lombardi

"People striving, being knocked down and coming back... that's what builds character. I've seen very little character in players who never had to face adversity." - Tom Landry

"You don't get any medals for trying. You're supposed to do that." - Bill Parcells

"If one's reputation is a possession, then of all of my possessions, my reputation means the most to me..." - Arthur Ashe

"Never underestimate the heart of a champion." - Rudy Tomjanovich

Expectations

Expectations - the act or state of expecting

There are two very important things about expectations that you need to know. You have to operate in a sense of expectancy and that expectancy is good, but you also have to understand that selfish motivations will not always allow the best result to come to fruition.

You have to operate with a sense of expectancy. Then when the time comes, you can step up because you have planned on being there all along. The surprise and the shock can be minimized because you have played this scenario through in your mind time and time again.

My father always said, "If you expect to fail, you usually do. On the other side of that, if you expect to succeed, you usually will." He was a man who believed in being positive. He talked often of expecting things in life and having that expectation spill over into our lives to a point that the expected seemed more or less, a given.

For many kids in the neighborhood in which I grew up, the conversations about life, education and success were centered on the high school diploma. That became, in many cases, the end of the line; the light at the end of the tunnel. The conversation in my house from the earliest of times could be heard as, "When you finish college…" From the earliest of times, I simply thought that I would have the opportunity to start my own life at the conclusion of college. Of course, through the blessing of athletics, I was able to go about my college education a bit easier financially than my brother and sister.

When it came to athletics, I expected to perform and perform well. Did my expectations always turn out the way I planned? Not at all!

Did I always have the proper expectations? Absolutely not!

Operating in a sense of expectancy will allow you to more clearly see your vision, communicate that vision to others and allow you to experience small victories on your way to the main prize.

Expect to plan and re-plan.

Expect to struggle.

Expect pain.

Expect to experience hard times.

But most of all…

Expect success.

Expect victory.

Expectancy in victory is derived from belief; a belief in a program, a system, a coach, a partner or a person.

Sports on expectations…

"When I first got here, they told me that I just needed to be competitive. When I was competitive, they wanted me to win. When I won, they wanted me to win them all. When I won them all, they said they meant by a bigger score." – Lou Holtz

"Achievement is largely the product of steadily raising one's levels of aspiration . . and expectation." - Jack Nicklaus

"Every time I stepped on the field, I believed my team was going to walk off the winner, somehow, someway." - Roger Staubach

"We're supposed to be perfect our first day on the job and then show constant improvement." - Ed Vargo

"You live up - or down - to your expectations." - Lou Holtz

"Other people may not have had high expectations for me…but, I had high expectations for myself." - Shannon Miller

"Visualize what you need to do. See it. Dwell on it. It'll happen. You can make it happen." - Marv Levy

"People don't care about how rocky the sea is, they just want you to bring the ship in." – Lou Holtz

"Gentleman, this is a football. Before we're through, we're gonna' run down everybody's throats." - Vince Lombardi

"See your future, be your future." - Caddyshack

"All these people expect a miracle; you have to create your own miracle." - Lance Armstrong

"I don't think I had any expectation other than wanting to win the championship." - Chan Gailey

Courage

Courage - mental or moral strength to venture, persevere, and withstand danger, fear, or difficulty

I have always found it interesting how we separate ourselves from issues of the day. Country singer Garth Brooks called it, "Standing outside the Fire." He said, "Life is not tried, it is merely survived, if you're standing outside the fire." Teddy Roosevelt said of this attitude, "Far better it is to dare mighty things, to win glorious triumphs, even though checkered by failure, than to rank with the poor spirits who neither enjoy much nor suffer much, because they live in the gray twilight that knows not victory nor defeat."

In one of my favorite movies, *The American President*, President Sheppard (Michael Douglas) operates under the following premise, "Fight the fights you can win." In one of my favorite parts of the movie, Martin Sheen says, "You don't fight the fights you can win. You fight the fights that need fighting." The issue is that what needs fighting is not always the easiest.

When I was in graduate school I got the opportunity to take up the game of golf. I was working a few hours per week in the cart barn at a local country club. Golf is a game, not unlike basketball, football and most other sports, where you have to call on your courage to do something that you normally do without thinking because of the extraordinary circumstances that occur. You might be hitting a shot towards a target that you cannot see. If you are me, you might find yourself hitting out of sand, high grass or water. You have to have courage and trust that you can make the shot and that the result will be tilted in your favor.

Having the courage to give it your all knowing that you are not 100%

Having the courage to give it your all when all the odds are against you

Having the courage to step up when the fate of your game is in your hands

Do you have the courage to expose yourself? Do you have the courage to invest everything into your craft? While it takes courage to start anything, it takes a multiple of courage to "sell out" to something. Can you disregard personal gain for the good of the team? Can you see the picture and commit to it. When I talk about selling out, I'm talking about a level of commitment that goes beyond your personal goals and even beyond your personal opinion. It is a level of commitment that needs courage because it relies on trust and faith in the greater good. That greater good of course being the team.

Can you sell out?

Can you look your teammates in the face and tell every last one of them that you are going to sell out for them?

Do you have the courage to be the best you can be?

You have to understand that one of the by-products of having the courage to sell out is that you find out the truth about yourself. Can you take that? Even if you do all that you can do and you truly sell out, you might find that it still was not enough. You will find out, as will your teammates and fans, that on this night, in this tournament, on this court, in this opportunity selling out was not enough.

That possibility, even the probability of that happening at some point cannot deter you. The opportunity to excel, to accomplish and to create a special happening in your life must take the lead in your decision making process.

It takes courage to be on the inside.

It takes courage to expose yourself.

It takes courage to try.

If you want to try, even to thrive instead of merely surviving, you can't stand outside the fire.

Have courage and step in.

Sports on courage…

"Whenever two teams or players of equal ability play; the one with the greater courage will win." - Pete Carrill

"You learn you can do your best even when it's hard, even when you're tired and maybe hurting a little bit. It feels good to show some courage." - Joe Namath

"Success is never final. Failure is never fatal. It's courage that counts." - Sam Rutigliano

"Courage is not the absence of fear, it is the conquest of it." - Anonymous

"Courage means being afraid to do something but still doing it." - Knute Rockne

"Courage is a special king of knowledge: from this knowledge comes an inner strength that subconsciously inspires us to push on in the face of great difficulty. What can seem impossible is often possible with courage." - Anonymous

"Show me a guy who is afraid to look bad, and I'll show you a guy you can beat every time." - Lou Brock

Leadership

Leadership - the act or an instance of leading

I think back to the 1999 NCAA National Championship football game where the "sick" skills of Michael Vick encouraged ESPN to get biblical when they did a pre-game segment on him.

The story starts with *"... a little child shall lead them. Isaiah 11: 6 – 9."*

Leaders come is all different shapes, sizes and attitudes. There are a number of characteristics that can be found in most leaders though...

Leaders work hard – Whether they are the first to practice and the last ones to leave or they spend their time in the film room, leaders work hard. Leaders are often the people who know both their assignment and the assignments of others. They work hard to a point that they act as a sponge and unconsciously work through the entire process to gain a level of expertise.

Leaders set an example – Be it their work ethic, the knowledge of their trade or the way they carry themselves away from the field or court, leaders set examples. Even when they may not be the most talented, the best skilled or show the most potential, leaders separate themselves from the average person.

Leaders know how to motivate – Leaders know that different people are motivated by different things and in different ways. Leaders can differentiate and learn how to move people to action. Even action above the perceived limits of their ability, a leader can find those things that motivate and make the group stronger by maximizing the ability of each individual.

Leaders know where they are going – Leaders know where they are going and have a strategy to get there. Their strategy could boil down to wanting it more than their opponent but there is always a strategy. "Where they are going" makes no reference to money, titles or championships although those things are acquirable goals. "Where they are going" could be from the scout team to actual playing time. It could be from the cut list to making the team.

Leaders show up – At the end of the day, leaders show up when the gym is dark, when the morning breaks and when the lights are their brightest. They show up when they are sick, when they are hurt, when they don't feel like it and they even show up when they are not getting the playing time they want. They show up even when it may just be a learning process because they are not close to being a major player. They show up because at that point in time, when they are called to step up, to be a part, to take their spot in the line up they will be prepared and can maximize their opportunity in hopes of gaining more.

In the movie *Drumline*, the band director is asking his percussion section leader about why he chose him to be the section leader. The section leader replies, "Because I liked the sound of the line more than the sound of my own drum."

That is what it takes.

You have to know how to follow before you can learn to lead. If you want to lead, you have to be willing to take a back seat. You have to be willing to encourage and nurture growth and the development of people around you without always having your name on the bright lights of the marquee.

Leaders may not make the most money.

Leaders may not be the most talented.

Leaders simply believe in the greater good and their opportunity to add to it.

Sports on Leadership...

"Having the capacity to lead is not enough. The leader must be willing to use it." - Vince Lombardi

"Personnel determines the potential of the team. Vision determines the direction of the team. Work ethic determines the preparation of the team. Leadership determines the success of the team." - John C. Maxwell

"The greatest thing in the world is to be able to have people count on you." - Lou Holtz

"Leadership, like coaching, is fighting for the hearts and souls of men and getting them to believe in you." - Eddie Robinson

"Leaders are like eagles... they don't flock. You'll find them one at a time." - Knute Rocke

"It is essential to understand that battles are primarily won in the hearts of men. Men respond to leadership in a most remarkable way and once you have won his heart, he will follow you anywhere." - Vince Lombardi

"Be enthusiastic as a leader. You can't light a fire with a wet match!" - Unknown

"Contrary to the opinion of many people, leaders are not born. Leaders are made, and they are made by effort and hard work." - Vince Lombardi

"You never find satisfaction among restless men -- and you never find leaders unless they are restless men." - Keith Jackson

"Leaders understand the power of choice." - Anonymous

"Leadership is a matter of having people look at you and gain confidence, seeing how you react. If you're in control, they're in control." - Tom Landry

"There are no warlike people, just warlike leaders." - Ralph Bunche

"Leadership is getting someone to do what they don't want to do, to achieve what they want to achieve." - Tom Landry

"Every leader needs to look back once in a while to make sure he has followers." - Anonymous

"Part of becoming a good leader is listening and learning." - Joe Montana

Potential

Potential - existing in possibility: capable of development into actuality

The world is full of potential. You would be hard pressed to find anyone in which you could find no potential. Does potential come in different levels and in different forms? Sure, but potential is there in every one of us. I see potential National Football League (NFL) tight ends and defensive ends all over my television during college basketball season and on the road watching high school games around the state of Texas. They don't understand that 6'7" guys grow on trees for the National Basketball Association (NBA). They were able to play in the middle in high school and down low in college, but 6'7" guys with marginal ball handling skills and no outside shot won't make it in the NBA. Many of these guys could have taken that size, strapped on a helmet and taken the football field by storm. So what makes people different? Sure, people have different potential in different areas but why isn't everybody good or successful at something?

The short answer is that potential is useless.

Potential alone, not unlike intentions, is pointless. Potential only informs us of our gifts. It only informs me of what I might be good at. It only informs me of what I might have a constitution to perform. It only tells me what my size and structure might lend itself to.

I remember being in grade school and hearing my science teacher talk about energy. There was potential energy and kinetic energy. While potential can always make you smile, kinetic energy pays the bills and gets it done.

There was a young man named Jeff that I heard about during his junior year in high school. I knew that we were recruiting him during his senior year. He was from a town right outside of the city I was in so we got to hear about his exploits all the time. My roommate saw him play in a high school football game one night and commented to me, "That's a bad white boy." Unimpressed like most upperclassmen with a resume, I only smiled mildly when he signed a national letter of intent to come to our school. He was playing football and running track and as I got to know him during football season, I can say that I liked him. I openly called him "country" but I liked him a lot. When track season rolled around, we spent a lot of time together training and running. We shared the same events and he worked himself onto a leg of our relay team. He managed to make it to the NCAA National track and field meet on the relay team and performed very well. He even made All American as part of that relay team. After a great transition year from high school to college and performing so well during his freshman year, the future was so bright for this kid that he gave it away and quit. During the year, he talked about this girlfriend. He even talked about the fact that they were serious. We never got the full story past the crowd of rumors but I never saw him again after the NCAA National Meet at the end of May.

I am the first one to say that people need to do what they have to do because at the end of our life, we are accountable for the gifts, talents and abilities that we have been blessed with. We are responsible for taking those gifts, talents and abilities and maximizing our lives and doing something good. We are not all successful with that all the time and I acknowledge so many shortcomings in my life that I could write a separate book.

But...

I, like everyone else, hate to play the 'if' game. I have had questions about decisions that I have made and with the understanding that hindsight is 20 / 20, you sometimes realize that you had sight the whole time; you just did not want to see it. I wonder if Jeff has played the 'if' game. I wonder if he is pounding himself with questions.

- I wonder what might have happened if I had stayed in school and got that free education.

- I wonder what might have been if I kept training and kept playing football.

- I wonder where I might be if I had finished my college degree.

I don't know where Jeff is today, but I hope and pray that he does not have these questions filling his head, and if by chance they are, I hope he can move on.

Potential is a great thing. You really can't start anything good without potential. We all have to take this potential that we have and turn those gifts, talents and abilities into something that can help us and help other people. Potential is just that, a start. Potential is a set of tools. Those tools still have to be used, improved and honed in order to bring about results.

Do not waste your life being "potential."

Sports on potential...

"I can't believe that God put us on this earth to be ordinary." - Lou Holtz

"The measure of who we are is what we do with what we have." - Vince Lombardi

"The function and duty of a quality human being is the sincere and honest development of one's potential." - Bruce Lee

"The more I train, the more I realize I have more speed in me." - Leroy Burrell

"All men are created equal but after that, it's up to you." - Jerry Lavias

"My faith leads me to look at what a person is capable of becoming and not just at his misdeeds." - Tom Osborne

"There are 86,400 seconds in a day. It's up to you to decide what to do with them." - Jim Valvano

"Don't measure yourself by what you have accomplished, but by what you should have accomplished with your ability." - John Wooden

"Don't matter if the cornerback is small, speed will make him seven feet tall." - Eddie Robinson

"Guys who know who they are usually turn out to be the best players in the NFL. Know what you can do and what you cannot do." - Bill Parcells

"It's one thing to be young and promising and another thing to be good." - Ken Dryden

Desire

Desire - to long or hope for; to express a wish for

You have got to want it!

When the clock is ticking down and your basketball team is down by one with 10 seconds left in the game, where are you?

When the game is closing and victory is 20 yards away because a field goal doesn't help you, where are you?

When it's two outs in the bottom of the ninth with the winning run on second, where are you?

When the game is tied and victory or defeat will be determined by a series of penalty kicks, where are you?

When you get the stick on the anchor leg of the 4 x 400 meter relay and you have two places to pick up to ensure your team the championship, where are you?

Scenario after scenario can be played out and the question still remains, where are you? I remember playing baseball in the backyard with my father and brother and them creating the scenario for me. They would be pitching and calling out the situation – bottom of the ninth, two outs, three balls and two strikes, go ahead run on second base. In their own way, they were trying to set me up for a possible, if not probable, situation that could present itself later in life. I remember living in that moment in high school and college sports and succeeding but I also remember having that opportunity to step up and not finding success.

Desire and stepping up are interchangeable. When you have the desire to succeed, you are volunteering to be the hero and/or the goat. That space on the marquee that shines so brightly with your name when you do something good becomes an easy and visible target when things do not pan out quite the way you planned. While you do assume some responsibility when you want the last shot or want the anchor leg, you open yourself to ridicule and failure because you might miss the shot. You might run a personal best on your anchor leg and still not get the job done for your team.

For all of the highlights that you see of Michael Jordan ending a game with a great drive or great shot, he has probably missed more game winning shots than he has made.

The jury is still out as to whether desire can be taught or coached but like most things, your desire can grow out of frustration. Desire, not unlike size and strength, has to be nurtured and sometimes has to be moderated. Your desire could grow because you discover that you enjoy something very much. Your desire could increase because of life circumstances such as a death, financial implications or a relationship.

Regardless of where you get it, get it! While some athletes experience some success without a lot of talent, without a lot of strength and without a lot of money, desire is the characteristic that cannot be absent if you want to experience success.

If you don't WANT it, you won't get it!

I was in Nashville in 2004 at a sports writer's conference and was in the hotel fitness center about to run on the treadmill when I saw something interesting outside of the hotel. My room window, as well as the windows on the outside of the fitness center, looked out over the meager football stadium of Southeastern Conference member Vanderbilt University. Looking into the open end of the stadium, there was a black top surface near one of the goal posts. In that area was open space and a chair. Also in that area was a young lady and a basketball. I thought to myself, it's June, very hot and months away from the October tip to basketball season. The young lady was dribbling back and forth down the length of this blacktop that was equivalent of the end zone for the football field. She was dribbling around the chair that sat in the middle. I could tell by her skill that she was a "real" basketball player. Back and forth, back and forth and then I decided to make it my business to meet her. I watched her workout for a few minutes. I walked out of the hotel and found a way into the stadium and as sad as it is, I interrupted her for a minute. She wore long black and gold shorts that were reminiscent of the sports programs at Vanderbilt. I confirmed that she did play for the university and asked her where there might be a pick-up game or two on campus. She even took out the time to ask if I was an athlete. She patronized me for a minute, gave me all the information that I requested and even invited me to play where she was playing. After the five minute exchange, I went back to the treadmill to spoil myself in the air conditioning to stay in shape. I decided to go the gym at five and as her work would help determine, she was one of the better players. She also appeared to be one of the hardest workers on the court with the rest of the nationally ranked Vanderbilt women's basketball team. I found out later that this young lady was Erica. It was the only time I talked to her, and that short stretch of time that I saw her play was the last time I saw her.

Regardless of where her career went on the court, her desire to excel as well as maximize her own talents will help her through the remainder of her life. While she, undoubtedly, experienced success on the hardwood, her desire to do well and reach her own goals will pay dividends in every other aspect of her life.

Sports on desire...

"The difference between a successful person and others is not a lack of strength, not a lack of knowledge, but rather in a lack of will." - Vince Lombardi

"The one strongest, most important idea in my game of golf - my cornerstone - is that I want to be the best. I wouldn't accept anything less than that. My ability to concentrate and work toward a goal has been my greatest asset." - Jack Nicklaus

"Being hungry and executing is two different things." - John Gruden

"If you'll not settle for anything less than your best, you will be amazed at what you can accomplish in your lives." - Vince Lombardi

"Champions aren't made in gyms. Champions are made from something they have deep inside them -- a desire, a dream, a vision. They have to have last-minute stamina, they have to be a little faster, and they have to have the skill and the will. But the will must be stronger than the skill." - Muhammad Ali

"I've always felt it was not up to anyone else to make me give my best." - Akeem Olajuwon

"Desire is the key to motivation, but its determination and commitment to an unrelenting pursuit of your goal -- a commitment to excellence -- that will enable you to attain the success you seek." - Mario Andretti

"Winners must have two things, definite goals and a burning desire to achieve them." - Brad Burden

"I learned that if you want to make it bad enough, no matter how bad it is, you can make it." - Gale Sayers

"Really, it comes down to philosophy. Do you want to be safe and good or do you want to take a chance and be great." - Jimmy Johnson

Teamwork

Teamwork - work done by several associates with each doing a part but all subordinating personal prominence to the efficiency of the whole

My father was a man of the 60's and 70's. In fact, he progressed nicely from birth but got to the 70's and jumped off the train and hung out in the 70's for the rest of his life. My father was king of the suede hat, blue jean jump suit and shirts with the butterfly collars. If you were in the San Francisco bay area during that time, you knew about Sly and The Family Stone. My parents turned me on to them and I heard a song by them that changed my life, "Everybody is a Star." My father took a liking to that song and for a long time referred to me as his little star. Anybody that personally knows me knows that I like stars and I owe a lot of it to my father.

Is everybody a star? Does everybody want to be a star? Are you a star if you are just a cog in a grand machine?

The people that I have always admired on a team were the walk-ons in college. They are kids that play for nothing but their love of the game and for the university. While most of the players on a college team are deciding who they are going to live with, many times, walk-ons are trying to decide if they can afford a place to live, if they can qualify for grants and where they can work part-time in the off season. They, more than most, understand the concept of teamwork. The walk-on athlete knows that this is their last serious team experience. They know that the odds are against them, even more so than the scholarship athletes, to play on a professional level. They rarely, if ever, log meaningful minutes during competition and sometimes don't even get quality time in practice. The most important part that most walk-ons understand is that their real contribution is on the scout team where they do everything they are told and practice long and hard without complaining to help the stars play better.

When you see your favorite team finish a season, on the good side or the bad side, take a look at the stars and then take a look at the walk-ons. Win or lose, it is usually the walk-on who feels it most. The stars will face another foe. For the walk-on, they walk away with no acclaim and probably to never don another team uniform outside of a city league or church league team. They walk away, just as they walked on but they leave with valuable life lessons in reliability, unselfishness, empathy, team work and the ability to be self-aware. They knew their place, and they were very proud of it.

All sports require a team, even if the actual competition is on an individual basis. Even in sports as individual as car racing, a team is present even though behind the scenes. There is a team of technicians making sure that the car is maximized. There is a group of sponsors who help make sure the team has the resources needed to maximize the car.

I have yet to see an all-everything quarterback who attained those levels of accolades by himself. There is someone catching those passes and scoring those touchdowns. There is a man on the sidelines who is calling the plays. There is someone on the practice field working on reading defenses, keeping the elbow up, recruiting the hips into the throwing motion and over-framing your target. There are a group of guys up front who protect him, block for him and help him up when he catches a hit. There is probably a young man right behind him that can run the ball and give the offense balance and allow the quarterback to work.

I have yet to see a great baseball player achieve everything inside of a bubble. There are hitting coaches, strength and conditioning coaches, fielding coaches, family members paying and transporting to and from practice as well as paying for those countless hours in the cage hitting pitches.

For every top basketball scorer, someone is passing the ball and getting the assist. Someone also paid for the AAU tournaments and bought more $100 pair of shoes that they care to talk about.

For every top golfer, there is a coach walking every hole with the golfer, someone buying clubs, paying dues and building mental toughness.

For every top skier, someone is buying lift tickets and equipment and someone is helping build the strategy for victory.

For every top setter, someone is paying for the cost of select teams and travel to tournaments along with someone on the outside who can spike it down the line.

For every top gymnast, someone is rising early in the morning so they have time at the gym. Someone is meeting them there to coach and develop them. Someone is organizing routines and calculating the difficulty.

Believe this because it is the truth…

There is no better feeling than being exhausted on your field of battle; lying on your back tired, sweaty and sore but victorious. There is no better feeling save for having a teammate who you have practiced, suffered and cried with lying next to you enjoying the same feeling.

Being part of a team is a beautiful thing. Whether your teammate wears your uniform and plays next to you or if your teammate is in the stands cheering for you, your teammates are invaluable to your success and your development.

Appreciate that! Your teammates, no matter what sport, how you get them or the value of their star-power will become lifelong friends for you and encourage you in so many ways outside of the realm of sports.

Sports on teamwork…

"People who work together will win, whether it be against complex football defenses, or the problems of modern society." - Vince Lombardi

"Great teamwork is the only way to reach our ultimate moments, and create breakthroughs that define our careers and fulfill our lives." - Pat Riley

"The achievements of an organization are the results of the combined effort of each individual." - Vince Lombardi

"Whether you like your role or not is not really relevant. What is important to understand is that we all have a role to play." - Lou Holtz

"One man can be a crucial ingredient on a team, but one man cannot make a team." - Kareem Abdul-Jabbar

"If a team is to reach its potential, each player must be willing to subordinate his personal goals to the good of the team." - Bud Wilkinson

"It is amazing what can be accomplished when nobody cares about who gets the credit." - Robert Yates

"The way a team plays as a whole determines its success. You may have the greatest bunch of individual stars in the world, but if they don't play together, the club wont be worth a dime." - Babe Ruth

"A team is where a boy can prove his courage on his own. A gang is where a coward goes to hide." - Mickey Mantle

"In basketball, you can be the greatest player in the world and lose every game, because a team will always beat an individual." - Bill Walton

"It seemed that there was often a synergy that enabled a group of players to exceed their combined talents." - Tom Osborne

"We've done so much with so little for so long, we believe we can do anything with nothing." - Marino Casem

"The strength of the team is the players and the strength of the players is the team." - Vince Lombardi

"Sure, basketball's a team game. But each player has a man to break down. A guy that's his to get around. And while it's true there's no 'I' in TEAM, consider this: There is an 'I' in WIN." - Nike

"Players win games, teams win championships." - Bill Taylor

Winning

Winning - to gain in or as if in battle or contest; to be the victor in

Dick Schapp once said about Michael Jordan in comparing him with Wilt Chamberlain – "Wilt Chamberlain seemed almost embarrassed by winning and Michael Jordan seemed hugely embarrassed by anything less than winning."

During my college years I frequently used (and occasionally still use) a sports term for how I dealt with issues in my life. It was very likely that you might hear me say, "I'm trying to win." I used this term in regards to my education, my relationships, my future career and of course in my athletic endeavors.

Winning – that's what it's all about. No matter what anyone tells you about team, community, camaraderie, trying hard and doing your best, sports, not unlike life, is about winning.

It is about winning, nothing else matters. Regardless of what good folks tell you to moderate your level of disappointment when things may not pan out quite the way you like, sports and life is about winning. We've all heard the sayings…

"It doesn't matter whether you win or lose it's how you play the game."

"Winning isn't everything."

"Sports are about fun, not winning."

"Everybody gets to play."

"As long as you try hard, that's all that counts."

In the words on my college track coach, "That's crap!"

When I talk about winning, you have to understand that I speak of winning in very broad terms. Winning as most people determine it is confined to the scoreboard of a sports competition or in a board room of a company.

I would suggest that winning reaches many more aspects of our lives than that. In the high school football movie, "*All the Right Moves*," Tom Cruise suggests to a college coach, "I don't think the NFL has any room for short white kids but I can get it done at the college level. I'm looking to trade my body for an education and still be able to walk in the end." In that scenario, he wins if he can get that education and stay relatively healthy.

Winning for me surely meant breaking the tape but also doing everything I could to maximize the talent and blessings I received. Part of that was using my scholarship to complete my education.

If you cannot control your weight, you don't REALLY want to win!

If you are not taking care of business in the classroom, you do not REALLY want to win!

If you are "smoking spliffs" and/or drinking your life away in your spare time, you don't REALLY want to win!

If your teammates cannot count on you to step up, play smart and play hard when it's crunch time and the pressure is on, you don't REALLY want to win!

If you cannot be timely, punctual and be where you are supposed to be when you are supposed to be there, you don't REALLY want to win!

If nothing is ever your fault and you have more excuses than answers, you don't REALLY want to win!

If you don't really want to win, don't front like you do.

If you are there for a letter jacket, conversation starter, to pay the bills or to pick up girls, do your thing but don't think that your teammates and coaches don't know. Don't think that they don't know that you are not a hard worker. Don't think that they don't know that you are selfish. Don't be surprised when it comes down to crunch time and at that point when you really want it, they don't have faith in you and you won't get your time to shine.

Sports on winning...

Training his nine-year old son, Mark: "How many lanes in the pool, Mark?" "Six." "How many lanes win, Mark?" "One." - Mark Spitz

"Some of us will do our jobs well and some will not, but we will be judged by only one thing-the result." - Vince Lombardi

"Winning--it's everything in sports. No matter how many times we've said, or have been told, 'It's not whether you win or lose, its how you play the game,' we all want to win." - Sandy Stiefer

"Winning ain't no fluke. We got down and got dirtier than they did." - John Thompson

"I may win and I may lose but I will never be defeated." - Emmitt Smith

"Without winners, there would be no civilization." - Woody Hayes

"If I were playing third base and my mother were rounding third with the run that was going to beat us, I'd trip her. Oh, I'd pick her up and brush her off and say, 'Sorry, Mom,' but nobody beats me." - Leo Durocher

"The only yardstick for success our society has is being a champion. No one remembers anything else." - John Madden

"Winning is not a sometime thing: it's an all the time thing. You don't win once in a while; you don't do the right thing once in a while;

you do them right all the time. Winning is a habit. Unfortunately, so is losing." - Vince Lombardi

"Winning isn't everything. Wanting to is." - Catfish Hunter

"Once you start keeping score, winning is the bottom line. It's the American concept. If not, it's like playing your grandmother, and even then you try and win – unless she has a lot of money and you want to get some of it." - Al McGuire

"We all choke. Winners know how to handle choking better than losers." - John McEnroe

"Winning is the science of being totally prepared." - George Allen

"What distinguishes winners from losers is that winners concentrate at all times on what they can do, not on what they can't do. If a guy is a great shooter but not a great skater, we tell him to think only about the shot, the shot, the shot - never about some other guy out skating him. The idea is to remember your successes." - Bob Butera

"I firmly believe that any man's finest hour, the greatest fulfillment of all that he holds dear, is the moment when he has worked his heart out in a good cause and lies exhausted on the field of battle-victorious." - Vince Lombardi

"You can't be a winner and be afraid to lose." - Charles Lynch

"The ultimate victory in competition is derived from the inner satisfaction of knowing that you have done your best and that you have gotten the most out of what you had to give." - Howard Cosell

"Why did I want to win? Because I didn't want to lose!" - Max Schmelling

"All right Mister, let me tell you what winning means - you're willing to go longer, work harder, and give more than anyone else." - Vince Lombardi

"A winner rebukes and forgives; a loser is too timid to rebuke and too petty to forgive." - Sidney J. Harris

"Only a man who knows what it is like to be defeated can reach down to the bottom of his soul and come up with the extra ounce of power it takes to win when the match is even." - Muhammad Ali

"Only winners are truly alive. Winning is living. Every time you win, you're reborn. When you lose, you die a little." - George Allen

"Winners don't blame fate for their failures nor luck for their successes. They know that a goal is only as worthy as the effort that's required to achieve it." - Unknown

"Winning is what life is all about." - Chuck Fairbanks

"When we lose, I can't sleep at night. When we win, I can't sleep at night. But when we win I wake up feeling better." - Joe Torre

"I'd like to be remembered for winning…If it's worth playing; it's worth paying the price to win." - Paul 'Bear' Bryant

Preparation

Preparation - the action or process of making something ready for use or service or of getting ready for some occasion, test, or duty

Tiger Woods and Jerry Rice are famous for their careers in golf and football respectively. Tiger Woods was, while still in his 20's, in search of number 18. Eighteen is the number of Major Championships won by Jack Nicklaus. Tiger's eyes as well as the eyes of the golfing world are fixed on that record and the possibility, if not probability, that Woods will get there. Jerry Rice is widely known as the best wide receiver to ever play the game of football. The dynasty of the San Francisco 49ers during the 1980's and early 1990's counted him as a major factor in attaining that status. Rice's story is only enhanced by the fact that he came from tiny Mississippi Valley State University, the historically black college in Itta Bena, Mississippi.

What do we always hear? They make their game look easy. Jerry Rice is the perfect wide receiver. Tiger outmatches anyone that he plays against.

There have been countless books and countless television stories about the relationship between Tiger and his father, Earl Woods. We know about Tiger sitting in a high chair while Earl hit ball after ball. We know about the hours on the driving range and seemingly insatiable need for success that has surrounded Tiger

Woods. Tiger has been seen at the course practicing for hours before he played and even after playing great is still seen on the range before a final round.

There have been stories on each and every sports channel on television about the summer regimen of Jerry Rice. They have broken down his hill training. They have shown his teammates whom he recruited into his training course. They have even shown athletes who were rehabilitating injuries taking on Jerry's hill.

When you hear the credo that nothing is easy, that is right. Tiger Woods and Jerry Rice both prove that point.

When you hear that Lance Armstrong is a natural…

When you hear that Nolan Ryan was able to pitch so long because he had the perfect throwing motion that allowed for efficiency and less wear and tear on his arm…

When you hear that the Kenyan distance runners just have natural ability…

When you hear that Kobe Bryant, Payton Manning and Eli Manning just have good pedigree…

When you hear the nonsense that race plays a part in what sports an individual seems to find success…

Don't believe that hype. Natural ability only plays a part in whatever activity someone finds a measure of success in. I won't even downplay pedigree and size factors but the ability to excel in sports is not something that can be passed down through DNA. You may have the talent and you may have the size but work and preparation still rule the day. How many seemingly great athletes do you see playing ball in the park as opposed to playing in an arena? How many 6'4", 270 lbs. kids do you see walking the hallways at a high school instead of at football practice? Talent and potential still have to meet the almighty "preparation" at some point.

Side note: Preparation is not limited to your sport or endeavor. Preparation includes the classroom, your lifestyle and how you treat your body. In short – Who cares if you are in top physical condition and ready to be All American if you don't take care of business in the classroom and are not eligible to play?

Better yet: for the high school athlete – Who cares if you run for 3000 yards and 25 touchdowns if you cannot meet the minimum basic requirements according to the NCAA to get a scholarship? It really doesn't matter. I hope your letter jacket with all your patches can get you a job because it won't get you an education. Only preparation does that.

Remember; if you fail to prepare, you prepare to fail.

Sports on preparation…

"One day of practice is like one day of clean living, it doesn't do you any good." - Abe Lemons

"They call it coaching but it is teaching. You do not just tell them… you show them the reasons." - Vince Lombardi

"When I played with Michael Jordan on the Olympic team, there was a huge gap between his ability and the ability of the other great players on that team. But what impressed me was that he was always the first one on the floor and the last one to leave." - Steve Alford

"If you don't invest much of yourself, then defeat doesn't hurt very much and winning isn't very exciting." - Dick Vermeil

"Champions do not become champions when they win the event, but in the hours, weeks, months and years they spend preparing for it. The victorious performance itself is merely the demonstration of their championship character." - T. Alan Armstrong

"The harder you work, the harder it is to surrender." - Vince Lombardi

"The fight is won or lost far away from witnesses -- behind the lines, in the gym and out there on the road -- long before I dance under those lights." - Muhammad Ali

"If you train hard, you'll not only be hard, you'll be hard to beat."
- Herschel Walker

"The will to win is important, but the will to prepare is vital." - Joe Paterno

"It's not necessarily the amount of time you spend at practice that counts; it's what you put into the practice." - Eric Lindros

"The will to win is not worth a nickel unless you have the will to practice." - Unknown

"If you don't do what's best for your body, you're the one who comes up on the short end." - Julius Erving

"The formula for success is simple: practice and concentration then more practice and more concentration." - Babe Didrikson

"You play the way you practice." - Pop Warner

"What I've been doing in practice will carry over into the game." - Randall Cunningham

"Ingenuity, plus courage, plus work, equals miracles." - Bob Richards

"They may outsmart me, or be luckier, but they can't outwork me." - Woddy Hayes

"The road to success is always under construction." - Unknown

"Success is like anything worthwhile. It has a price. You have to pay the price to win and you have to pay the price to get to the point where success is possible. Most important, you must pay the price to stay there." - Vince Lombardi

"Spectacular achievements come from unspectacular preparation." - Roger Staubach

"The dictionary is the only place where success comes before work." - Unknown

"I found this sandbank by the Pearl River near my hometown, Columbia, Mississippi. I laid out a course of 65 yards or so. Sixty-five yards on sand is like 120 on turf. But running on sand helps you make your cuts at full speed. I try to pick the heat of the day to run in, but sometimes that sand will get so hot you can't stand in one place. It'll blister your feet. You get to the point where you have to keep pushing yourself. You stop, throw up and push yourself again. There's no one around to feel sorry for you." - Walter Payton

"I've never known a man worth his salt who in the long run, deep down in his heart, didn't appreciate the grind, the discipline. There is something good in men that really yearns for discipline." - Vince Lombardi

"I hated every minute of training, but I said, 'Don't quit.' Suffer now and live the rest of your life as a champion." - Muhammad Ali

"Good athletes prepare themselves to play, but more importantly, prepare themselves to WIN!" - Michael Lasher

"If you wanna' get better, concentrate on the areas you'd rather not. Force yourself to work the weak link. Physically. Mentally. But most of all, repeatedly." - Nike

"The legs feed the wolf." - Herb Brooks

Confidence

Confidence - the quality or state of being certain

Confidence means something different to everyone. What one might call confident, another might call arrogant. Being certain, being confidant and being sure is a trait that EVERY successful athlete or successful person, for that matter, possesses.

In the 2005 college football season, The University of Texas went on the road to play a Top 5 ranked Ohio State team. During some of the loudest times of the game, the Texas defense was waving their hands in the air at the Ohio State fans essentially telling them, "Make all the noise you want. We are going to make plays." Texas went on to hold Ohio State to five field goals in that game and allow quarterback Vince Young to make a play near the end of the game to win the game for the University of Texas.

Confidence is not about pounding your chest.

Confidence is not about running your mouth.

It is about the way you carry yourself.

It is about how you carry yourself in the huddle. It is about how you carry yourself in the dugout, on the court, in a meeting or in a boardroom.

It's about facing your opponent, even in the midst of struggle, giving him a wink, a smile or a pat on the helmet just so he knows that his work is not done.

It's about being confident enough to be humble.

Are you confident enough to play a role on a team and allow someone else to leverage their skills and be the hero?

Are you confident enough to cheer? Can you enjoy the moment even though the spotlight is not on you?

Confident people are comfortable in those situations.

Be confident in what you do. Be confident in what you do well. Most of all be confident in your ability to be flexible, to stretch beyond your own scope, to learn and to thrive in adversity.

Now let's talk facts. You can have all the confidence in the world. You can have confidence in your skills and you can have confidence in your ability to perform. None of that is worth a bucket of warm spit if the people around you do not have confidence in you.

Are the people around you confident not only in your skills but in your ability to perform when the time comes?

Do your coaches have confidence that you will do the things off the field to maintain your place on it?

Do your coaches have confidence that when times get tough, you will show your strength and not lose control and make matters worse?

Do your coaches have confidence in you to make the play when it counts most?

7th inning, 2002 College World Series, Texas vs. Stanford, bases empty and the score tied 5 – 5, University of Texas centerfielder Dustin Majewski hits a 3 – 0 pitch into the right-center field seats. Dustin goes around the bases, not cheering, not clapping, not pumping his fist, but chewing and popping his gum. He was confident in his ability and captured the moment. The Longhorns go on to win that semifinal game 6 – 5 before winning the National Championship over South Carolina. Dustin not only had confidence in himself but the very conservative 'manufacture the run' coach in Augie Garrido had enormous confidence in him in order to allow him to swing away with a 3 – 0 count.

Sports on confidence...

"It's not bragging if you can back it up." - Muhammad Ali

"If they playing football, I'm gonna' make it." - Paul "Tank" Younger

"Somebody has to be the hero. It might as well be me." - Charles Barkley

"There is a difference between conceit and confidence. A quarterback has to have confidence. Conceit is bragging about yourself. Confidence means you believe you can get the job done. I have always believed that I could get the job done." - Johnny Unitas

"Emotion is what makes me what I am today. It makes me play bigger than I am." - Charles Barkley

"I was told over and over again that I would never be successful, that I was not going to be competitive and the technique was simply not going to work. All I could do was shrug and say 'We'll just have to see'." - Dick Fosbury

"If you are struggling offensively, there is no other option; you better get on my back and ride this thing all the way home." - Keyshawn Johnson

"Each Warrior wants to leave the mark of his will, his signature, on important acts he touches. This is not the voice of ego but of the human spirit, rising up and declaring that it has something to contribute to the solution of the hardest problems, no matter how vexing!" - Pat Riley

"You need to play with supreme confidence, or else you'll lose again, and then losing becomes a habit." - Joe Paterno

"Confidence doesn't come out of nowhere. It's a result of something... hours and days and weeks and years of constant work and dedication." - Roger Staubach

"Besides pride, loyalty, discipline, heart, and mind, confidence is the key to all the locks." - Joe Paterno

"It's lack of faith that makes people afraid of meeting challenges, and I believed in myself." - Muhammad Ali

"Before you can win, you have to believe you are worthy." - Mike Ditka

"I make plays!" - Charles Woodson

"Confidence is a very fragile thing." - Joe Montana

"To be a champion, you have to believe in yourself when nobody else will." - Sugar Ray Robinson

"Confidence is a lot of this game or any other game. If you don't think you can, you won't." - Jerry West

"I am the greatest." - Muhammad Ali

"One important key to success is self-confidence. An important key to self-confidence is preparation." - Arthur Ashe

"I never doubted my ability, but when you hear all your life you're inferior, it makes you wonder if the other guys have something you've never seen before. If they do, I'm still looking for it." - Hank Aaron

"When you're as great as I am, it's hard to be humble..." - Muhammad Ali

"There are times when you're tired and times when you don't believe in yourself. That's when you have to stick it out and draw on the confidence that you have deep down beneath all the doubts and worries." - Jim Abbott

Competition

Competition - a contest between rivals; active demand by two or more organisms or kinds of organisms for some environmental resource in short supply

While I believe in playing sports for the love of the game, I have grown weary of what I like to term as the softening of America. It seems that more and more young people, not only athletes, are taught…

Some is enough…

Everyone can succeed…

Try and that will be enough…

This is even more confounding to me when I think about the people in society who are revered like Michael Jordan and Tiger Woods. If you took a poll, you would find that most people would love for their children to have the success, at their trade, that Michael Jordan and Tiger Woods have at theirs; but if society were any indicator of the public forum, they would not like what it takes to get there. Everyone has read about Michael Jordan's competitive nature in pick-up games as well as practice. Tiger Woods has held eight shot leads and was still the last person on the practice range. Tiger Woods has played so well that his competition has said…

"The only real question is longevity, there are a lot of issues regarding longevity; desire is a big one. But, that doesn't appear to be an issue for him because his target is Jack Nicklaus. He wants to set all the records."

"It just looks like the only thing he is driven to do is be the best golfer, not of just our time but maybe of all time."

In the 100th U.S. Open in 2000, Tiger Woods took the lead in the first round and never relinquished it. He showed after having a 10-stroke lead after the third round that you never stop competing. You might have to change what you compete against but you always compete. There was a point (probably sometime in the first nine holes of the final round) that Tiger Wood's competition was not the rest of the competitive field. His competition had become the record book and some of the records that were set more than 100 years before he walked the course at Pebble Beach that weekend.

Competition is a part of life. You will compete for jobs, education, housing, and relationships. It does not matter if "Soft Hearts" tell you that you don't have to keep score, it's all about having fun, doesn't matter the outcome, as long as you try, do not believe them. Sometimes, you have to learn to try harder and try smarter. You will compete in every aspect of your life. You will compete to make athletic teams, band chairs, academic teams, scholarships, spouses, and jobs. Let's look at a few examples...

#1 - At some juncture you might be competing to keep your job. The nationwide layoffs of thousands of people in the last five years were about competition. If a department has five people and they need to lay one of those people off, do you think they are going to line everyone up in alphabetical order and lay off the last one in line? How about laying off the shortest one, or the tallest? How about laying off the ugliest one? No, they are going to lay off the person that they can easiest do without. In short, they will layoff the least productive one. Every day you are on your job is a day to compete with your co-workers. Understand that!

#2 – Wide Receiver A is 6'3", 200 lbs. and runs 4.4 seconds in the 40-yard dash. He finished his junior season with 49 catches for 904 yards and eight touchdowns. Wide Receiver B is 6'2", 200 lbs. and runs 4.4 seconds in the 40-yard dash. He finished his junior season with 35 catches for 805 yards and 11 touchdowns.

Wide Receiver A carries a 3.3 GPA, scored 990 on the SAT and won the Team Player Award at his team banquet. Wide Receiver B carries a 2.2 GPA and did not get a school admitting test score on the first two attempts but did get a better score on the second time and feels that the third time is the charm.

More - Wide Receiver A is very respectful and gracious in conversation and the coaches seem to love having him in the program. Wide Receiver B was playing video games during conversations, was hardly ever at home during the week when called, had six personal fouls and was held out of starting one game and suspended for two games due to discipline problems.

When a college coach is looking at both players and trying to think about which player he would like to be around and coach for four years, what decision do you think he is going to make? No coach wants to recruit a kid who he will have to be on constantly to go to class, make his grades and stay out of trouble.

Let's keep it real, a 6'3", 200 lbs., 4.4 running trouble maker will always have a place to play because the end game is getting better and a coach will agree to take a project or two (or more) if he can score touchdowns.

Before you believe the myth that people are born with a competitive spirit, understand that might be true but competition, the tenets of competition, the virtues of competition are a learned attitude and process. Lee Janzen may have put it best in the aforementioned 2000 U.S. Open when he said about Tiger Woods, "It's almost like he trained for this; like he's won it before in his mind so many times that it's just a foregone conclusion, in his mind, that he's going to win."

Competition is a good thing; one of the best things. Competition has been the catalyst for invention, success and people doing more than ever thought possible. Competition is a spirit, a prevailing attitude and a virtue of Americana that took man to the moon, brought down the price of computers, led man to fly and of course has taken sports to the forefront of society.

Don't let people who are scared to compete taint your mind into thinking that competition is a bad thing. The world is a much better place because competition exists. Capture it, thrive on it and experience victory.

Sports on competition…

"For years, I have said my motivation for playing wasn't for fame and fortune, but rather the love of competing." - Mark McGwire

"I don't hate anyone, at least not for more than 48 minutes, barring overtime." - Charles Barkley

"The principle is competing against yourself. It's about self-improvement, about being better than you were the day before."
- Steve Young

"Competition is what made America great." - Jim Foster

"I love the winning, I can take the losing, but most of all I love to play." - Boris Becker

"If my mother put on a helmet and shoulder pads and a uniform that wasn't the same as the one I was wearing, I'd run over her if she was in my way. And I love my mother." - Bo Jackson

"You may not be in a class by yourself, but it sure doesn't take long to call the roll." - Bum Phillips

"You don't play against the opponent; you play against potential and perfection." - Lee Corso

"If you can't win, make the fellow ahead of you break the record."
- Unknown

Goals

Goals - the end toward which effort is directed

As a young athlete, I remember my mother asking me what I wanted to do athletically. When I revealed some pretty lofty hopes she simply made the statement, "Hope is not a strategy."

One thing that I always wanted to attain was to be called an All American. I made it a point to figure out a strategy to get me there. When I started my freshman year of track and field in college, I asked a very simple question, "What does it take for me to be All American?" I was informed that I would need to place in the top six at the NCAA Indoor National Meet and in the top eight at the NCAA Outdoor National Meet.

I then asked what times (in general terms) it took in my events to become All American. When I got that answered, the only thing that I needed to know was who on my team ran those 'All American' type times. When I found that individual, I had a new training partner and I wanted to learn what I could from him. I think he understood my desire and he helped me with anything that I ever needed. Sure he had his own interest at stake because I also ran on a relay with him, but he helped bring me along and assisted in socializing me to collegiate track and field.

This same sentiment of strategy helped me later in life when I was done with athletics and putting my degrees to work. Whether it was trying to do "it" better than other people and finishing assignments before due dates or figuring out how and when I could finish this book, strategy building that was forged in sports helps me everyday in life.

Building a strategy to accomplish things and reach goals allowed me to reach goals in sports, life, family and relationships.

It can do the same for you.

Remember, hope is not a strategy!

How can you sit in the car without having a destination? How productive would it be to hit a golf ball with no target in mind? Of course we are talking about goals. Your goal is your target.

Start Small

There are not many things worse in goal setting than setting a goal so high and so big without leaving steps in the middle as action items to reach the big goal. You will learn to value goals that are achievable. Being able to set small goals and reach them and those goals being part of the big picture will give you more success and also find you achieving at a higher level than you are accustomed to.

Write them down

You need to be able to see your goals. You need to be able to read them. Place little reminders in your house or in your car. Place notes of encouragement to yourself in your locker or on your screensaver. Things that you think about and read will stick in your mind and will allow you to consciously work towards them.

Be Specific

Your goals have to be specific. The most important part about your goals being specific is that they need to be performance based goals and not outcome goals. You want to set your goals in a way that you have as much control as possible. There is nothing more dispiriting than not reaching your goals due to things that are out of your span of control. Goals that you set toward outcomes are left open to failure because of things that are beyond your control.

"I want to be rich," is not a goal. Rich is relative and also does not give you a target that you can reach for and breakdown into smaller goals along the way.

"I want to be the best quarterback in the state," is not a goal. It might be a desired recognition but in the end is out of your span of control because that is a subjective opinion by people who may or may not have seen you play. A goal in this situation would be…

"I want to complete 68% of my passes, throw for 3000 yards, run for 1000 yards and have a 5 to 1 touchdown to interception ratio." That is an individual goal. On a side note, your goals, in most ways, need to tie in with the big picture. In this case, the team goals might be to win 14 games and win a state championship.

Be real

It has always amazed me that people cannot even be real with themselves when creating goals. In many cases, they are the only one who knows what the goals are and they still seem unrealistic. You know yourself better than anyone else. You know what you are willing to do, what you are willing to endure and if you have the talent to reach the level you set for yourself. With that being the case, only you can set goals that are realistic for your skill-set, talent level and the observed need for your skill.

Sports on goals...

"All winning teams are goal-oriented. Teams like these win consistently because everyone connected with them concentrates on specific objectives. They go about their business with blinders on; nothing will distract them from achieving their aims." - Lou Holtz

"Take a minute: look at your goals. Look at your performance. See if your performance matches your goals." - Dan Kelly

"Always have a plan and believe in it. Nothing good happens by accident." - Chuck Knox

"If you set a goal for yourself and are able to achieve it, you have won your race. Your goal can be to come in first, to improve your performance, or just finish the race. It's up to you." - Dave Scott

"If you are bored with life, if you don't get up every morning with a burning desire to do things - you don't have enough goals." - Lou Holtz

"Setting a goal is not the main thing. It is deciding how you will go about achieving it and staying with that plan." - Tom Landry

"Take dead aim." - Harvey Penick

"You never get ahead of anyone as long as you try to get even with him." - Lou Holtz

"Nothing is as real as a dream. The world can change around you, but your dream will not. Responsibilities need not erase it. Duties need not obscure it. Because the dream is within you, no one can take it away." - Unknown

Coaching

Coaching - to instruct, direct, or prompt; to train intensively

There are two things that seem to be incontrovertible about coaching.

1. Games are usually won by the coach with the best players on his team.
2. Every really good coach is also a teacher.

I have always admired coaches. They have to be able to motivate, discipline, teach and calm, sometimes all within a couple of hours. Coaching is not an easy thing because everyone has different motivations, even coaches.

Another characteristic that most coaches possess is that they are never satisfied. Many of them develop this trait over time even if they don't possess it when they start coaching. They usually develop it because the people around them; the people who support the coach and their team are never satisfied.

Lou Holtz said of his coaching jobs...

"When I got there, they wanted me to be competitive. When I was competitive, they wanted me to win. When I won, they wanted me to win them all. When I won them all, they said, "We meant by a big score!" You are never going to be able to satisfy people.

The success of any coach is the result of what you see on the field of play or in their place of competition. Believe whatever you want to believe but those are facts. Coaches are responsible for two things and two things only:

- Winning
- Presenting an opportunity to members of a team

Winning

Coaches have to win. They do not only want to win, they have to win. I have never heard of a coach who was run out of town because he won too much. Even when a coach is not what he should be off the field, winning will usually give him an extended stay. Of course when the winning is done, the coach is usually close behind.

Many coaches are complete in their job because they are good coaches, good examples and good teachers. Many coaches are looked at as mentors and almost second parents. These coaches are an extra blessing because they bring so much more to the table than sports.

Winning is important, sometimes the most important thing. Winning takes on a whole different meaning when coaches win and win the right way. The right way being with class and good people while educating and teaching young people.

Opportunity

The greatest thing that any coach brings to the life of a young person is a number of opportunities. These opportunities are what make many coaches get up in the morning. Coaches allow young people to be a part of something bigger than the individual. They get to be part of a group with one goal. Coaches allow young people to stretch and to reach goals many never thought possible. Coaches push and motivate a group of individuals toward being a winning team.

Through the process of building a team, the individual is formed. This formation is part of what allows the individual to become what they are destined to be. This is consistent regardless of the status within the team and goes beyond the life of the team. That the individual was part of the team is the principal that remains regardless of success years after the team experience ends.

The things mentioned above are all great things but the thing that many coaches allow the opportunity to learn are the tools that help make you successful. The tools and the characteristics that make you a success in football, basketball, softball, soccer, track and field, baseball, golf or any other sport are the same tools that will help you succeed in life. Coaches afford young people those opportunities. Many times these coaches are the only people who can offer these opportunities to young people and the appreciation is shown usually in the reverence with which the coach is treated.

Choice

If we operate with the understanding that coaches are paid to win, we also understand that during the job of coaching, coaches offer opportunities to young people. The only thing that is left unfinished in regards to coaches is that opportunities are not very different than potential.

If a coach offers you the opportunity to get a free education of your choice, learn discipline, a sport, to be a team player, to persevere, to learn practice habits and to learn how to win, the responsibility still falls on you to choose to take that in and apply it across the board in your life.

We all have friends or family who made the wrong choice and left a lot on the table. Essentially a coach, in conjunction with the institution and the rest of the staff, set a feast for you. The feast consists of an education, the characteristics of winning, the joy of success and the fun that is always associated with winning.

Whether you sit down and take full advantage of it is up to you. The coach can only set the table for you. If you don't eat and find yourself extremely hungry years after the feast was set, then that was your choice and your youth cannot be an excuse.

Every coach goes about it in different ways. You have some coaches who scream and curse and some who hug and cry. Both types of coaches are successful and for different reasons. I have had some incredible men in my life and they, too, have been coaches of teams that I have been on. That includes coaches in high school, college and in my professional life away from sports.

The fact still remains that many dentists, doctors, attorneys, businessmen, teachers and all different career people attribute much of their success to their coaches and their athletics.

What kind of influence are you?

No pressure!

Sports on coaching...

"I never thought about the records. I just thought about the kids. When they come out of Grambling they have my signature on them. They aren't the English teacher's kids or the Math teacher's kids. They's Eddie's boys and I'll try to make them better than average." - Eddie Robinson

"One of the biggest problems you have when you take over a losing situation and I did it six different times is that everybody is saying that guy should have been the coach or he should have been the coach. Players are talking. I'd walk in and I'd say to them, 'Men, I know you didn't choose me. You would never choose me because I'm tough and there's going to be a lot of changes made. But I want you to understand this though, I chose you. I came here because I believe you can be special. I believe this place can be special.'" – Lou Holtz

"The other day somebody asked me what I would want on my tombstone. I told them it should say, "I'd rather be coaching." - John Gagliardi

"It's my way or the highway and my way is hard." – Don Haskins

"I never criticize a player until they are first convinced of my unconditional confidence in their abilities." - John Robinson

"80% of games are won by the coach with the best players on his sideline." – Lee Corso

"It's just a game. But, I love it!" - Herman Boone

"There is a difference between spirit and temperament. It is a slight difference, but it is an important one. I valued players with spirit and avoided those who were temperamental." - John Wooden

"I like Friday night when we're looking for a win. I like Saturday morning when we've found one." – High School Coach

"The only thing that disturbs me about my profession is the fact that people give you too much credit when you win and too much criticism when you lose. I'll be the same person and do the same things and say the same things when we lose. But people won't believe me then. I won't change, but the people will." - Darrell Royal

"It's not my job to hold down the score, it yours!" - Bobby Bowden

"Any time you give a man something he doesn't earn, you cheapen him. Our kids earn what they get, and that includes respect." - Woody Hayes

"It's not my job to motivate players. They bring extraordinary motivation to our program. It's my job not to de-motivate them."
- Lou Holtz

"My hobby is my work. I love it so much, it is not work." - Dick Vermeil

"But it's still a coach's game. Make no mistake. You start at the top. If you don't have a good one at the top, you don't have a cut dog's chance. If you do, the rest falls into place. You have to have good assistants, and a lot of things, but first you have to have the chairman of the board." - Paul "Bear" Bryant

"My wife goes to church and prays for me. I tell her to pray for you guys. You need more help than I do." - Joe Paterno

"You got a hundred more young kids than you have a place for on your club. Every one of them has had a going away party. They have been given the shaving kit and the fifty dollars. They kissed everybody and said, 'See you in the majors in two years.' You see these poor kids who shouldn't be there in the first place. You write on the report card '4-4-4 and out.' That's the lowest rating in everything. Then you call 'em in and say, 'It's the consensus among us that we're going to let you go back home.' Some of them cry, some get mad, but none of them will leave until you answer them one question, 'Skipper, what do you think?' And you gotta' look every one of those kids in the eye and kick their dreams in the ass and say no. If you say it mean enough, maybe they do themselves a favor and don't waste years learning what you can see in a day. They don't have what it takes to make the majors, just like I never had it." - Earl Weaver

"If you make a game a life - and - death proposition, you're going to have problems. For one thing, you'll be dead a lot." - Dean Smith

"What it comes down to is that anybody can win with the best horses. What makes you good is if you can take the second or third best horse and win." - Vicky Aragon

"People are in greater need of our praise when they try and fail, than when they try and succeed." - Unknown

"First of all, we've got to have a basic understanding of who's in charge around here. There can never be a question of that. Well, I am the new guy around here. I'm the head coach. And in the past three years your Florida State football team has managed to win only four games and in the meantime lose twenty-nine. Y'all have tried it your way, and where did it get you? Nowhere. Now, I think I know how to win. And from now on at Florida State we're gonna' do things my way. If you don't like it, then hit the door. Go somewhere else, because if winning doesn't mean something to you then we don't need you. From now on, it's going to be an honor to wear a garnet jersey and represent Florida State University. We're gonna' win again at Florida State." - Bobby Bowden

"Coach to win!" - Dan Hawkins

"Either love your players or get out of coaching." - Bobby Dodd

"My responsibility is to get my twenty-five guys playing for the name on front of their uniform and not the one on the back." - Tommy Lasorda

"You might reduce Lombardi's coaching philosophy to a single sentence: In any game, you do the things you do best and you do them over and over and over." - George Halas

"You inspire loyalty, not demand it." - Tom Jackson

"It is better to build strong children than to try to repair adults." - Unknown

"The country is full of good coaches. What it takes to win is a bunch of interested players." - Don Coryell

"I often told my players that, next to my own flesh and blood, they were the closest to me. They were my children....I always tried to be fair and give each player the treatment he earned and deserved." - John Wooden

"Praise Loudly. Criticize Softly." - Lou Holtz

"If a man is a quitter, I'd rather find out in practice than in a game. I ask for all a player has so I'll know later what I can expect." - Paul "Bear" Bryant

"But coaching was all I ever wanted to do." - Eddie Robinson

"As coaches and as parents, we can only teach our kids that life is a series of options, just like football. If you make good decisions, you are likely to succeed." - Mack Brown

"To me, the coaching profession is one of the noblest and most far-reaching in building manhood. No man is too good to be the athletic coach for youth." - Amos Alonzo Stagg

"I can only show you the way. It's up to you to go there." - Larry Ellis

"You ask players to come 1,500, 2,000 miles away from their home basically because they trust you. It's very hard then, when things don't pan out quite the way you like, for you to then abandon them." - Tom Osborn

"People don't care how much you know until they know how much you care." - Willard Tate

"If anything goes bad, I did it. If anything goes semi-good, we did it. If anything goes really good, then you did it. That's all it takes to get people to win football games for you." - Paul "Bear" Bryant

"Coach's open the door. You enter by yourself." - Unknown

"Most coaches study film when they lose. I study film when we win – to see if I can figure out what I did right." - Paul "Bear" Bryant

"We're gonna' coach like our hair is on fire and we expect them to play the same way." - Brent Venables

"You coach to win; you play to win. Anything less than that is unacceptable." - Tyrone Willingham

"Don't ever ask a player to do something that he doesn't have the ability to do, because he'll question your ability as a coach, not his as an athlete." - Lou Holtz

"I try to get a piece of every boy that plays for me, and I try to give him a piece of me if it's worth anything." - Eddie Robinson

"You are what your record says you are." - Bill Parcells

Perspective

Perspective - the capacity to view things in their true relations or relative importance

I have had some people in my life who offered great perspective that showed me things dealing with competition and dealing with life. Perspective is a very broad word. It can come to us in any of 100 ways. We just have to be receptive to it and even invite it in and allow ourselves to be better. These times allow for us to reflect and realize different things that make us better athletes, better teammates and better people.

When I got to Abilene Christian University, Aaron was already there. He was a sprinter with a great resume who hailed from Caracas, Venezuela. He had participated in many international competitions and had faired pretty well. I believe he had also been an Olympian representing his native country. Because of some things that I outline in the strategy section, I made it my business to get close to him. I got as close as a city kid from California could to an athlete from Venezuela who was at least ten years my elder. I feel safe in assuming that he thought I was a "hot head", talked too much and thought too much of myself even if he never said it to me. Nonetheless, he took an interest in me if for no other reason than the fact that I ran a leg on his 4 x 100 meter and his 4 x 400 meter relays.

During that same year in the final of the 400 meter race at the conference track and field meet, he (a senior) was in lane five while I was in lane four. After he took a pretty good lead on the field during the first 250 meters I was looking at his back and focusing on him when I started to gain ground. When coming off the last turn, I was moving up next to him and I heard in my right ear, "Take it, Sean!"

I don't know whether he was not feeling good. I don't know if he was tired from his previous events. I don't even know if he was hurt. I do know that those two words stuck with me and I will always remember them and appreciate Aaron and his encouragement that day. It was the only time that I ever beat him and I think winning that conference championship in that first year propelled me to greater heights.

It not only propelled me to greater heights in track and field but also offered me perspective in how we have the opportunity and even the responsibility to help, encourage and inspire the people around us.

From putting athletics in their proper place to managing our work/life balance in careers, gaining perspective on sports, life and relationships help broaden us as people and many times help us return to our base as to why we are the people we are.

Sports on perspective...

"Everyone has a plan until they get punched in the mouth." – Mike Tyson

"I know that I'm never as good or bad as any single performance. I've never believed my critics or my worshippers, and I've always been able to leave the game at the arena." - Charles Barkley

"Don't tell people your problems: 80% don't care; and the other 20% are glad you have them." - Lou Holtz

"Age is a question of mind over matter. If you don't mind, it don't matter." - Satchel Paige

"To me, there are three things we all should do every day. We should do this every day of our lives. Number one is laugh. You should laugh every day. Number two is think. You should spend some time in thought. Number three is, you should have your emotions moved to tears, could be happiness or joy." - Jim Valvano

"Inches make a champion." - Vince Lombardi

"We all have to play the ball as it lies." - Bobby Jones

"The only way I'd worry about the weather is if it snows on our side of the field and not theirs." - Tommy Lasorda

"Things turn out best for the people who make the best of the way things turn out." - John Wooden

"I don't consider people like Jack Nicklaus as heroes. I admire them for their golf. I guess my own role model is my dad." - Tiger Woods

"A life is not important except in the impact it has on other lives." - Jackie Robinson

"To the world you might be one person, but to one person you might be the world." - Unknown

"If I finish #2 at Notre Dame, everybody calls me an idiot, if I finish last in Medical School, they call me Doctor. Explain that one." - Lou Holtz

"Whoever said 'It's not whether you win or lose that counts' probably lost." - Martina Navratilova

"Make each day your masterpiece. You have control over that." - John Wooden

"The better you become, the more people will try to find something wrong with you." - Robert Lansdorp

"If what you did yesterday seems big, you haven't done anything today." - Lou Holtz

"You're either improving or getting worse; no one stays the same." - Ben Howland

"Baseball is the only field of endeavor where a man can succeed three times out of 10 and be considered a good performer." - Ted Williams

"You have to learn how to get comfortable with being uncomfortable." - Lou Piniella

"When you're riding, only the race in which you're riding is important." - Bill Shoemaker

"Yesterday is a cancelled check. Today is cash on the line. Tomorrow is a promissory note." - Hank Stram

"If you try to fight the course, it will beat you." - Lou Holtz

"I always turn to the sports page first. The sports page records people's accomplishments; the front page, nothing but man's failures." - Supreme Court Justice Earl Warren

"I don't care how good you play, you can find somebody who can beat you, and I don't care how bad you play, you can find somebody you can beat." - Harvey Penick

"Most games are lost, not won." - Casey Stengel

"You don't have to be an apple to recognize one." - Tom Jackson

"The greatest test of courage on the earth is to bear defeat without losing heart." - Ingersoll

"This was a great experience for the kids. Twenty years from now these guys will be sitting in some bar in Idaho drinking beer and talking about the time they went down and played Texas." - Utah State Coach Phil Krueger (after losing to the Longhorns 61-7 in 1975 on why Utah State would schedule a game with Texas)

"Life in the public eye is not without a price." - Tom Osborne

"It's just a job. Grass grows, birds fly, waves pound the sand. I just beat people up." - Muhammad Ali

"I always knew looking back on the tears would make me laugh but I never knew looking back on the laughs would make me cry." - Unknown

"Sure, luck means a lot in football. Not having a good quarterback is bad luck." - Don Schula

"You're never as good as everyone tells you when you win, and you're never as bad as they say when you lose." - Lou Holtz

"If size is all that matters, how come the whale is endangered and the ant continues to do just fine?" - Kelly Marshall

"Everyone likes a good loser, especially when he is on the opposing team." - Milton Segal

"A heavy hitter is nothing more than a little hitter who kept on hitting." - Pete Zafra

"You can't possibly hit the ball if you are thinking about all the possible ways you could miss." - Unknown

"Selfishness as long as not to the detriment of the team is fine." - Tom Jackson

"Competitive sports are played mainly on a five-and-a-half-inch court, the space between your ears." - Bobby Jones

"The best and fastest way to learn a sport is to watch and imitate a champion." - Jean-Claude Killy

"The truth is that many people set rules to keep from making decisions." - Mike Krzyzewski

Luck

Luck - the events or circumstances that operate for or against an individual

Luck is a tricky thing to think about and to understand. I have always defined luck as preparing yourself in every way so that when opportunities present themselves, you can take advantage of them.

I have often heard that when you accomplish anything big, some luck has to go along with it. Things sometimes just kind of go your way. A fumble happens to bounce right back into your hands instead of into the hands of the opposition. You just happen to hear that this job if going to be created before anyone else does and you start to position yourself for it. You happen to get season tickets right behind a guy that has the connections to help you get where you want to be. None of those things matter if you are not prepared when that bounce comes, you have not been prepared to take a new job or that chance meeting takes place.

Jim Tressel, Head Coach at Ohio State University, said something in 2003 that will stick with me forever. When asked how he would address his team before they played the University of Miami for the Football National Championship, he answered by saying, "We'll go out and play our game, play hard and see if, at the end of the night, we deserve to win."

When you ask most winning athletes who have faith in what they performed, they will say something like, "I did the best I can do and if someone beats that, then they deserve to win."

Now when we talk about deserving and luck, sometimes you can do all you can to set yourself up to be lucky. You might have done everything you can to feel that you deserve it. In the end you still might not win. The other team thinks that they deserve it as well. That is the beauty of sports and life. Even if you deserve to win, you still have to take it. That is why; at the end of the day, you have to be satisfied with doing your very best and see if you, at this time, deserve to win.

Did BYU earn the National Championship in 1984 by beating a 6 - 4 Michigan team in the Holiday Bowl. Absolutely not, but guess what? They got the trophy.

Did Tommie Frazier deserve the Heisman in 1995? He would have gotten my vote but in the eyes of most others, Eddie George deserved to win. Eddie got the trophy.

Does Nykesha Sales deserve to have the scoring record at the University of Connecticut? In my mind no, but she is in the record book.

Did Bill Buckner deserve to have that grounder go through his legs that fall day in 1986? Of course not! But, it happened and the whole city of Boston still blames him for not breaking the curse.

I'm sure you can think back to many negative things that have happened to you which you feel you did not deserve. You probably raise the questions yourself – Why me? How could this happen to me? We all have them. On the other side of that coin, many things have happened in my life that make me think the exact opposite. I have often raised the question, "How did I get blessed enough to be in this moment?"

More than things and/or possessions, I have had quality people come into my life and these quality people have added dimensions to my life that cannot be measured in dollars, cents or things.

In many instances, we get what we deserve. We get it whether we are blessed with it and are happy or hurt by it and have the opportunity to learn from it and get better. That, even when it sucks, is sports.

Funny part is; it is also life.

Sports on luck...

"You've got to think lucky. If you fall into a mud-hole, check your back pocket - you might have caught a fish." - Darrell Royal

"Luck? If the roof fell in and Diz (Dean) was sitting in the middle of the room, everybody else would be buried and a gumdrop would fall in his mouth." - Leo Durocher

"Luck is what happens when preparation meets opportunity." - Darrell Royal

"The more I practice the luckier I get." - Arnold Palmer

"Sometimes it's better to be lucky than good." - Unknown

"The sun don't shine on the same dog's butt all the time." - Catfish Hunter

"The champion makes his own luck." - Red Blaik

"Prepare yourself in every way you can by increasing your knowledge and adding to your experience, so that you can make the most of opportunity when it occurs." - Mario Andretti

Life

Life - the sequence of physical and mental experiences that make up the existence of an individual; an opportunity for continued viability

City leagues, semi professional leagues, $200 per-game indoor leagues, contact flag football leagues, car lots, track and field meets, etc. are full of people who didn't understand the balance of sports and life.

I stood on the infield of the Texas Relays in 2003 and ran into many runners who I ran against in college and post-college. Hanging around former athletes is much like hanging around people in the music business. When you happen to be around former stars or very popular people in the music business, the first thing to come out of their mouth is, "Yeah, I'm in the studio right now putting my CD together." You can't help but laugh when you hear it, at least I couldn't.

How many times have you heard a former athlete say, "That school didn't really care about me? They just wanted me to play my sport. They used me." That is another laughable moment. You will read in another section of this book that coaches, no matter what they tell you, are paid to win. It is YOUR responsibility to use this opportunity to better yourself for the long term. If you don't, you will be relegated to using your name and your 15 minutes (or four years) of fame to sell cars, boats or keep that 'worker-bee' job as long as you don't miss the basketball and softball league games, so you can make the office look good.

I know that sounds harsh, but you must get the point to maximize your opportunity to get a "top-shelf" education that, in many cases, you wouldn't have access to if you couldn't perform at a high level in athletics.

I could spend this time talking about the possibility and probabilities of a professional career but the odds are, you have already heard all of that.

Everyone that has this page open and is reading this book has air in their lungs and some portion of their life left to live.

It's on you.

Sports on life…

"If all I'm remembered for is being a good basketball player, then I've done a bad job with the rest of my life." - Isiah Thomas

"The game of life is a lot like football. You have to tackle your problems, block your fears, and score your points when you get the opportunity." - Unknown

"Don't go to the grave with life unused." - Bobby Bowden

"In doing your work in the great world, it is a safe plan to follow a rule I once heard on the football field: Don't flinch, don't fall; hit the line hard." - Theodore Roosevelt

"Be strong in body, clean in mind, lofty in ideals." - Dr. James Naismith

"Somebody will always break your records. It is how you live that counts." - Earl Campbell

"A trophy carries dust. Memories last forever." - Mary Lou Retton

"Football is like life -- it requires perseverance, self-denial, hard work, sacrifice, dedication and respect for authority." - Vince Lombardi

"Sports is life with the volume turned up." - Barry Mano

"Football was my salvation. I was always getting into trouble, but football helped me mature. I'm lucky I started playing football when I did." - Dat Nguyen

"Life is like boxing. You've only got so many punches to throw and you can only take so many." - George Foreman

"I owe sport a great deal. Not only has it enabled me to earn a comfortable living; it helped me grow." - Grantland Rice

"Looking back, it would be impossible for me to overstate the impact of sports in my life." - Spike Lee

"One afternoon, one moment in one life, can make a whole lifetime." - Keith Jackson

"Life is what happens to you while you're working for your future."
- Unknown

"Everyone will forget you when you leave the game, and all you will have left are the things that it has taught you – to sacrifice, to work hard." - Bum Phillips

Perseverance

Perseverance - in a state, enterprise, or undertaking in spite of counterinfluences, opposition, or discouragement; to go on resolutely or stubbornly in spite of opposition, importunity, or warning

"Struggle, survival; victory in defeat." That is a line attributed to Coach Herman Boone in the movie *Remember the Titans*. He talks about his love, his affinity even for the game of football. He called the football field his sanctuary.

It is easy to tell great stories of perseverance, of working hard, of sustaining through the pain and failure and finding victory in defeat. But I think it might be useful to approach perseverance from a standpoint of why we persevere.

Tom Osborne, the Hall of Fame former Nebraska football coach, talked about his desire to excel in sports which was partly driven by the fact that his father loved sports and he wanted to do things that his father enjoyed.

Perseverance, many times, can be used synonymously with motivation because it takes a certain motivation to persevere through anything. There is no perseverance without motivation. Motivation comes in several forms, such as:

Financial Motivation - There may be a possibility of a financial reward, contract or benefit that motivates you to persevere through rough times.

Title Motivation – Maybe you have always wanted to be a Captain, a Vice President or an MVP. Sure the titles come with other benefits, but the name, the possibility of the title is what moves you to continued action.

"I'll Show You" Motivation – Many people achieve great things because they were encouraged to conquer and persevere simply because someone told them they couldn't. The thought or action of someone being negative can be a huge motivator and can surely allow people to overcome huge obstacles.

Success Motivation – Some people want to be good at everything they try. These people just want to win whether it be a board game, a state championship game or the Saturday morning golf game with childhood friends. They will go through hard times and persevere because success in 'whatever' is the goal.

Love Motivation – When you love something, anything, you don't go to work. It's not really considered work. You are simply paying the price to do what you love. A true affection for something whether it be sports, business, music or anything else makes your job a lot easier and the ability to deal with, be motivated by and thrive on hard times that much easier.

What makes one person persevere makes another person quit. What makes one person take another step forward turns another person back. What is that motivation that keeps you going? What is past the goal line that you are reaching for which makes persevering worthwhile for you? This is the question you have to ask yourself. When you are in the throes of struggle, in the middle of problems, what puts a smile on your face and forces you to keep going?

Whatever motivates you to action, whatever motivates you to keep going, harness that motivation and turn it into something productive.

Take that sour lemon and make lemonade.

Sports on perseverance...

"It's not so important who starts the game but who finishes it."
- John Wooden

"They say that breaks even up in the long run and the trick is to be a long-distance runner." - Chuck Knox

"I've always made a total effort, even when the odds seemed entirely against me. I never quit trying; I never felt that I didn't have a chance to win." - Arnold Palmer

"Adversity causes some men to break; others to break records."
- William A. Ward

"There is no time to think about how much I hurt; there is only time to run." - Ben Logsdon

"You have to motivate yourself through pride. You must push yourself mentally and physically. A lot of people say John Havlicek never gets tired. Well, I get tired it's just a matter of pushing myself. I say to myself 'He's as tired as I am, who is going to win the mental battle?'" - John Havlicek

"Pain is weakness leaving the body." - Tom Sobal

"Nothing in the world can take the place of persistence. Talent will not: Nothing is more common than unsuccessful men with talent. Genius will not: Unrewarded genius is almost a proverb. Education will not: The world is full of educated derelicts. Persistence and determination alone are omnipotent." - Unknown

"When you're playing against a stacked deck, compete even harder. Show the world how much you'll fight for the winners circle. If you do, someday the cellophane will crackle off a fresh pack, one that belongs to you, and the cards will be stacked in your favor." - Pat Riley

"Perseverance isn't just the willingness to work hard. It's that, plus the willingness to be stubborn about your own belief in yourself." - Merlin Olson

"About all I did was stick with it." - Paul "Bear" Bryant

Have Purpose

Have Purpose - to hold or maintain as a possession, privilege, or entitlement something set up as an object or end to be attained

My wife is a runner in its truest sense of the word. I have heard stories of her beating all the boys at "Field Day" in elementary school. I have seen pictures of her running in middle school. I have seen videos of her running and winning a state championship in high school. I have seen her win races in college. She has run for personal glory, relay championships, and NCAA National Championships. I have seen situations where it was up to my wife to run better than she had ever run in order for the team to win. I have seen her excel in all of these situations and because she did, she was a collegiate All-American and has her picture on the wall in the coliseum at the university. She has pushed herself to the limit for the glory of God, her teammates, her coaches, her family and herself. However, her life changed after we got married. The first issue was that she was married to me and that is a tall order. She was a full-time teacher and coach. She had decreased her mileage to about 20 miles per week. She stopped running competitively. She talked about doing some 5K or 10K races. She had even tossed around the idea of running a marathon.

In early 1998, she came home and said, "On the first weekend of November, I want to go to Austin." We left that Saturday evening and drove the 3.5 hours to Austin. We got up Sunday morning and

Karen said we needed to leave by 7. She put on an old college Cross Country t-shirt, some shorts and her faithful Adidas. We got in the car and drove downtown. By the time we got there, it was raining pretty hard. She kissed me, got out of the car, started jogging and quickly disappeared over a hill. This was her first 5K in a long time. But this wasn't just any road race, she was #1394 and she was running in "The Race For The Cure." This was a race to be run to raise money to assist in finding a cure for cancer. We lost my wife's mother to cancer the previous December. About race time, I could barely get out of the car. It was a full-scale thunderstorm. I could barely see where I was driving. The next time I saw her she was soaked and smiling. She hugged me and said that she was cold. We got back to the car and she put on some layers and we drove out of downtown. Later that day as we were driving back home, I told my wife that I was proud of her and admitted to her that I, in a small way, was living vicariously through her during that race. Her mother and my father died within a few days of each other. I took that time to reflect on the memory of my father and the legacy he left for my brother, sister and I.

In a matter of minutes she was in a deep, peaceful sleep. This special woman, who has spent her whole life running, found a new reason to run. She wasn't running for a place atop the award stand, trophies, All-American certificates, watches, money, scholarships, or for personal glory. It was in memory of a mother, wife, and grandmother who lost her second battle with cancer. Many of the runners in the race had tags on their backs that said, "In celebration of..." for a person who is living with or did not die from cancer. My wife, along with many others, had a tag that said, "In memory of..." for those persons who were lost to cancer. In the middle of a thunderstorm, my wife found peace. Peace in the comfort that her mother is in a far better place; peace in the fact that by using her talents to help, she honors the memory her mother and all those who struggle daily with the dreaded disease of cancer. That might be the most valuable 3.1 miles she's ever run.

Sports on having purpose...

"Boys! The eyes of Texas are upon you. Texans are huddled around their radios from Brownsville to Wichita Falls, from El Paso to Texarkana, in every home, grocery store, drug store, barbershop and hardware store in the state of Texas all are eagerly waiting to find out how you do today. Today, you are not just representing the University of Texas, today, you're fighting and playing for the entire state of Texas! This is Texas against Wisconsin! Set your jaws! Make up your minds! Let's play a game that will live in the hearts and minds of the people of Texas FOREVER!" - Dana X. Bible (Texas coach's pre-game speech to the Longhorns prior to the 1939 contest with Wisconsin. Texas won 17-7 over the larger UW squad)

"Football is only a game. Spiritual things are eternal. Nevertheless, beat Texas!" - First Baptist Church, Feyetteville, Arkansas, circa 1980

"Outlined against the blue-grey October sky, the Four Horseman rode again. In dramatic lore they are known as Famine, Pestilence, Destruction and Death. These are only aliases. Their real names are Stuhldreher, Miller, Crowley and Layden." - Grantland Rice

"I don't know Rock. It's all right, I'm not afraid. Some time Rock when the teams up against and things are wrong, and the breaks are beating the boys; tell them to go in there with all they've got and win just one for the Gipper. I don't know where I'll be then rock, but I'll know about it and I'll be happy." - George Gipp

"The most fitting tribute that we could give them would be to have a great game, with great spirit, and great enthusiasm and a great display of what Texas A & M University is all about; that is the bond of the students to each other." - R.C. Slocum

"Our deepest fear is not that we are inadequate. Our deepest fear is that we are powerful beyond measure. It is our light, not our darkness that most frightens us. Your playing small does not serve the world. There is nothing enlightened about shrinking so that other people won't feel insecure around you. We were all meant to shine as children do. It's not just in some of us, it's in everyone. And as we let our own light shine, we unconsciously give other people permission to do the same, as we are liberated from our own fear. Our presence automatically liberates others." - Timo Cruz (The Movie - *Coach Carter*)

Opportunity

Opportunity - a favorable juncture of circumstances

Brian Griese will forever have a place in my head and be an encouragement to me.   He decided to walk on at the University of Michigan when nobody came calling to Columbia High School where Brian put up average high school passing numbers. After laboring behind a group of very good quarterbacks at Michigan, Griese found himself at a crossroad. He had opportunities to move on in life. He was about to finish his degree in Environmental Policy. Problem was, because he had red-shirted, he still had one year of eligibility left. He went back and forth and had conversations with his family about what he should do. After the Michigan head coach asked him to, "Come back and help us one more year," the player who spent his junior year divided between punting, field goal holding and some quarterbacking decided to play his last year. The year was 1997. During fall practice, injury and the good play of Brian gave him an opportunity to see the field. As he took this last year to grow into the position and the pressure packed role of quarterback at the University of Michigan, Griese found winning was getting easier, the season was fun and he was voted 1st team All Big 10 Conference by the media. They just kept winning behind the strength of a good defense and the offense led by this former walk-on. Near the end of the season the Wolverines of the University of Michigan found themselves ranked No. 1 in the nation and on a collision course with # 7 ranked Washington State of the Pacific 10 Conference. Washington State was led by Ryan

Leaf, another high profile quarterback and he would eventually be the #2 pick in the NFL draft.

The setup couldn't be better if Norman Rockwell had painted it. Brian Griese, the same young man who was looking for a place to play and had to be convinced to go back for his senior year was one Rose Bowl win away from leading his team to the National Championship. The cherry on top of the banana split was the fact that his father, former Purdue quarterback, Heisman trophy winner and NFL Hall of Famer was doing the color analysis for ABC with famed broadcaster Keith Jackson calling the action. After stellar defensive play and Griese playing the game of his life while passing for 251 yards and three touchdowns, the game seemed at hand when Washington State's last fruitless effort lead to the clock running out. When the clock ticked down to :00, the Wolverines had won their 11th National Championship and their first in 50 years. With the emotions of the day taking their toll on Bob Griese and his wife, who was in the booth with him as they watched Brian fulfill a family's hope and dreams, the envelope was handed to Keith Jackson and life at that moment was made even better. Keith Jackson said to the millions listening…

"The MVP of the 1997 Rose Bowl – you wanna' know who it is? I'm standing alongside his proud daddy. Quarterback Brian Griese of Michigan. What a year he's had; changed his whole life!"

When Bob Griese was finally able to speak, he muttered, "You almost lost me partner."

Keith Jackson closed the moment by telling him, "I don't blame you. You wanna' cry, you go ahead, I'll hold you up!"

Opportunities, despite what the world will tell you, don't come along all the time. Brian Griese's one decision to play his senior year changed his life. He has now made a life for himself in the

NFL. One moment, one opportunity, one chance can make a lifetime and a life for you.

Who knows what Brian Griese would be doing right now if he had not made the decision to return for his senior year?

One decision!

One opportunity!

The opportunities that present themselves to you might not always be as clear as you think they should be. Sometimes the opportunities come in the form of a problem or a bad circumstance. The difference between the successful athlete and continual failure is how you use those opportunities to enhance your life. You've got to take your lemons and make lemonade. Again, this is another piece of your life that is 100% up to you. How you act, how you react and how you finish will determine your ability to find success in life, whether it be sports, work or family.

Sports on opportunity…

"You'll always miss 100 percent of the shots you do not take." - Wayne Gretzky

"I never looked at the consequences of missing a big shot . . . when you think about the consequences you always think of a negative result." - Michael Jordan

"The man who complains about the way the ball bounces is likely the one who dropped it." - Lou Holtz

"Every shot not taken is a goal not scored." - Wayne Gretzky

"On a pass play, somebody's always open. I just have to find him." - Joe Montana

"How you respond to the challenge in the second half will determine what you become after the game, whether you are a winner or a loser." - Lou Holtz

Success

Success - favorable or desired outcome

What is success? Is success a lot of money? Is success based on possessions? Is success based on notoriety? Is success based on fame?

Success is something that is truly individual.

I worked at a very large computer company for a few years and the whole intent of the company was based on individual success and service. Each and every customer had different needs for their personal computer and could call the company and request a computer just for them. Whether they needed a small hard drive and mobile storage like USB drives or whether they needed a laptop with a DVD player for travel. Each customer could call in and drop a laundry list of needs and wants and this company could build a computer just for them. The company ensured, by this method, that each customer experienced a level of success.

Your life, your sport, your job, your relationships are all on an individual basis not unlike the computer company that I was a finance geek for. Each of us have different gifts, talents, abilities and loves and those things shape us, our environment, our life and our definition of success.

You must hunt down and find what your passions are. Find what your gifts are. Find what you are good at. Ask someone who you care about. Ask someone who cares about you: What am I good at? I remember asking my mother that very question. What do you think I can be good at? What are the strengths that I possess? What opportunities do I have to get better?

Once you have determined what your skills are, what your gift is, then it is incumbent upon you to work, sharpen and hone that skill into something that is great.

It only takes one thing. I am a firm believer in Malachi 3:10 when the verse ends with "… and I will pour you out a blessing that you won't have room enough to receive." It only takes that one blessing to open up a life of success.

Oprah Winfrey does so many things now from her show to charity work to makeovers to scholarships. It all started with one talent to report the news and do it passionately.

Michael Jordan has done a number of things in his life but they all got their start on the basketball courts of Wilmington, NC.

Of course these are special cases of people who took that one blessing and rode it all the way to greatness in the eyes of many. Success with your talent might be making the varsity basketball team as a senior or winning a forensics competition. Success might mean being able to obtain an athletic scholarship even though you know you may not have the tools to play at your sport's highest level.

Sports on success…

"It's 3 downs and a punt all of your life. You gotta' keep your head up because you never know when you gonna' break one." – High School Coach

"One day you're drinking the wine and another day, your stomping the grapes." - Lou Holtz

"The biggest thing that I felt basketball could do for me was help me get a good education." - Julius Erving

"To succeed…You need to find something to hold on to, something to motivate you, something to inspire you." - Tony Dorsett

"You can't just love the game when everything goes the way you want it to go." - Dennis Green

"He who stops being better, stops being good." - Oliver Cromwell

"Success without honor is an unseasoned dish; it will satisfy your hunger, but it won't taste good." - Joe Paterno

"Some people skate to the puck. I skate to where the puck is going to be." - Wayne Gretzky

"I am a big believer in the 'mirror test'. All that matters is if you can look in the mirror and honestly tell the person you see there, that you've done your best." - John McKay

"Without self-discipline, success is impossible, period." - Lou Holtz

"Sweat plus sacrifice equals success." - Charlie Finley

"Things turn out best for people who make the best of the way things turn out." - Unknown

"I've had enough success for two lifetimes, my success is talent put together with hard work and luck." - Kareem Abdul-Jabar

"Every success is built on the ability to do better than good enough." - Unknown

"When I was younger, I thought that the key to success was just hard work. But the real foundation is faith. Faith--the idea that 'I can do it'--is the opposite of fear ('What if I fail?'). And faith creates motivation which in turn leads to commitment, hard work, preparation...and eventually success." - Howard Twilley

"A man who wakes up and finds himself a success has not been sleeping." - Frank Lane

Failure

Failure - omission of occurrence or performance; lack of success; a falling short

I have always been amazed by, what I see as, the world's distorted view of failure. Failure is something that everyone, especially young people, should know about. It is not a bad idea to talk about failure. On the contrary, everyone should know the possibility and probability, with given circumstances, of failure.

You absolutely can fail and will fail if you do not take care of business. I tell all athletes that I work with, "Failure is an option and the most used option." The world, people, friends (take your pick) would like you to believe that there is a group of "haves" and "have nots" and you are destined to remain in the group to which you were born. Nothing is further from the truth.

As an athlete and all through life, I have run into people who voluntarily join the group hoping and understanding that they will fail. Sometimes they seem to not even know it but they show all the signs. They are always just trying to get by. I have heard from them and still hear from athletes today, "I have to get a C or D so I am eligible in the fall." When you talk with them some time later, they have changed their tune. It only takes one trip to a guidance counselor at a high school to understand why college coaches don't want to recruit them. That long walk to an advisor when you have exhausted your four years of eligibility, been eligible all (or most) of the time and find out you are a number of years short of your desired degree plan does the trick. Now that you have wasted the tutors, the teachers or professors willing to help, all of the assistance that you might need to get you to your end result, you lean on the athlete's favorite crutch, "That school didn't make sure that I graduated. All they cared about was that I stayed eligible and played. They used me!"

Let's get this one straight. No matter what a coach tells you, his responsibility is to win games, run a clean program and keep the money rolling in, regardless of the level of competition. High academics, graduation rates, high SAT scores, community service, high numbers and articulate athletes are icing on the cake. The coach may care about them on a high level but those virtues are not the reason a coach keeps his job. Coaches at most Division I and Division II schools keep their jobs by votes and the alumni and supporters vote with their wallets in donations and ticket sales. If icing on the cake mattered on the highest level, the coaching carousel would not turn every year.

Ask yourself if you would have been accepted to Notre Dame, Michigan, UCLA, Texas, North Carolina, Duke, Berkeley, Wisconsin, Georgetown or the other "Top Shelf" schools on your own merit? The first bell to go off in your head telling you that you have a special opportunity is when you have a 2.35 GPA with a minimal score on the SAT or ACT but get that acceptance letter from "fill in one of the above schools." Sure you can't major in what you want but you can get into the Liberal Arts school and be in some fine program like Community Studies. That should be the first bell for you that should let you know, you might be behind the curve in education but someone is willing to let you catch up because you can shoot a jump shot, catch a football or hit for the cycle.

When I was in college, I heard a few people say, "Those people are using you. You would not even be there if you weren't an athlete." My answer was always, "Well you may be right but we both have things that the other person needs. They need an athlete and I need an education."

At the end of the day, you are stuck with the question, when the lights go out and the stadium quiets, where are you? Have you put yourself in a position to go on to capitalize on your opportunity? Have you floated through school hoping to stay eligible as opposed to building a foundation for your future? Have you built the relationships you need to build to start some kind of career?

What you don't want is regrets. You will be overloaded with them if you don't take care of business on **AND** off the field.

Sports on failure...

"Never let the fear of striking out get in your way." - Babe Ruth

"The minute you start talking about what you're going to do if you lose, you have lost." - George Shultz

"One slip does not make a person forever a failure, any more than one good turn makes a person forever a saint." - Unknown

"People who are involved in life have experienced disappointment; they have experienced pain and they go on." - John Thompson

"That's why they make pencils with erasers." - John Mackovic

"Failure isn't so bad if it doesn't attack the heart. Success is all right if it doesn't go to the head." - Grantland Rice

"Sometimes you have to lose major golf championships before you can win them. It's the price you pay for maturing. The more times you can put yourself in pressure situations, the more times you compete, the better off you are." - Tom Watson

"Excuses are the nails used to build a house of failure." - Unknown

"You want to fail yourself? I don't have any problem with that. But don't cause other people to fail." - Lou Holtz

"I have always felt that although someone may defeat me, and I strike out in a ball game, the pitcher on the particular day was the best player. But I know when I see him again; I'm going to be ready for his curve ball. Failure is a part of success." - Hank Aaron

"Your IQ will grow through frustration." - Joe Dumars

"Losers never know why they are losing. They will mention injuries, the officiating, the weather and bad breaks." - George Allen

"We were running on bloody stubs because we kept shooting ourselves in the foot." - Jeff Van Gundy

"Fear not that your life will someday end. Fear only that you do nothing with it." - Unknown

"I never thought of losing, but now that it has happened, the only thing is to do it right. That's my obligation to all the people who believe in me. We all have to take defeats in life." - Muhammed Ali

"Some of the greatest heroes are those people that made mistakes and were able to handle it." - John Thompson

Perform

Perform - implies action that follows established patterns or procedures or fulfills agreed-upon requirements and often connotes special skill; implies a complete realization of ends or possibilities

Get it done! Performing means different things to different individuals. Performance to some means that you are maintaining a daily regimen in the way you live, the way you work and the way you operate. Performance to others means that you raise the level of your performance when the lights are at their brightest and the scrutiny at its most intense.

I am a huge Tiger Woods fan. Though grudgingly, he did earn the respect of his peers, and sometimes that respect led players in 2000 to say the following things about him...

"I'm just thankful they don't pay only one spot every week."

"He might win 100 tournaments."

"What we ought to do is look at what is going on and recognize that Tiger Woods is probably the greatest athlete in sports and he's playing our sport"

"If you're looking to challenge him as far as a career is concerned, find a new sport."

"He has set the bar so high he's the only one who can jump over it."

"Motivates me to maybe check his schedule and play the other tournaments. It's almost demoralizing to tee off on Sunday morning 18 shots behind knowing that I wasn't a total hack for three days, but knowing that I had no chance."

I will never forget the 2000 Players Championship. It had been proven time and time again that player after player folded when up against Tiger Woods on the last day of a tournament. Hal Sutton was playing in the final group and had told anyone who would listen that he would not be intimidated by playing against Tiger Woods. I like most thought, "Yeah, good lip service." What he did that day made me a believer and taught me more about stepping up and being a performer.

Hal Sutton was one stroke up when he and Woods approached the Par 4, 18th hole at the TPC at Sawgrass. Hal Sutton understood that he didn't have to be the best ever. He didn't have to have the major championships. He didn't have to be the No. 1 ranked player in the world. He did not have to be the leading money winner on the PGA Tour. He had to be the best player on Sunday of the Players Championship on March 26th, 2000. His statement at the time and the commentary that followed gave me great insight into performance. As he hit his iron shot on the 72nd and last hole of the tournament he said, "Be the right club, today!" The numbers bear out the fact that Hall Sutton does not always hit the best iron shots, the best drives, the best putts or post the lowest scores. Tiger Woods was ranked higher than him in virtually every category that the PGA keeps statistics on. He knew that he only needed to be the best on this shot. His understanding of that allowed him to focus and that focus lead that shot to be right. He won that tournament and cemented his quote in the minds of a lot of sports fan, myself included.

Performing is about stepping up; being on the main stage and loving it. If you want to perform, you have to want the ball in your hands with time running out and you need two to tie and three to win. If you want to perform, you have to want the baton on the anchor leg of the relay and let it all come down to you. If you want to perform, you have to tell the coach to give you the ball on the one-yard line. When the game is on the line, you have to want the pressure and thrive on it.

Sports on performing…

"Don't be a spectator; don't let life pass you by." - Lou Holtz

"If we play well we're gonna' win. If we don't play well, we don't have a chance. It's up to us to perform well. You can't perform well if you're afraid or if you're nervous about making a mistake. This is a time to just go out there and put on a show." – Lou Holtz

"Big time players make big plays on big days!" - Santana Moss

"Concentration is the ability to think about absolutely nothing when it is absolutely necessary." - Ray Knight

"Someone has to step up and be the hero." - Augie Garrido

"Let's just do what we do and see what happens." - Dave Perno

"My job is to give my team a chance to win." - Nolan Ryan

"Players make plays. Plays don't make players." - Bill Walton

"Sometimes you have to suck it up and call a number." - Darrell Royal

"If I had stood at the free-throw line and thought about 10 million people watching me on the other side of the camera lens, I couldn't have made anything. So I mentally tried to put myself in a familiar place. I thought about all those times I shot free throws in practice and went through the same motion, the same technique that I had used thousands of times. You forget about the outcome. You know you are doing the right things. So you relax and perform." - Michael Jordan

"When you've got something to prove, there's nothing greater than a challenge." - Terry Bradshaw

"Be the right club, today." - Hal Sutton

"Beat your opponent where he is strongest and you demoralize him." - Vince Lombardi

"Play like a champion today." - Unknown

"The measure of an athlete is how he performs under duress." - Mitch Albom

"When you do call an audible, make sure it works." - Otto Graham

"You can only change your reputation on the field." - Joe Montana

"Run to the football and knock somebody out." - Ray Lewis

"Dance with the one that brung ya'." - Darrell K Royal

"When the game is over, I just want to look at myself in the mirror, win or lose, and know I gave it everything I had." - Joe Montana

"Power is not revealed by striking hard or often, but by striking true." - Honore de Balzac

"You don't play for the people in the stands. You let the people enjoy watching you play." - John Thompson

Fun

Michael Jordan is one of the people that I think of when I think about someone who enjoyed their game.

ESPN once said of Michael Jordan, "He was having fun, you knew it, and he knew you knew it."

I understand the evolution of sports and the financial beast sports have become and the corresponding pressure that goes along with it; but sports, athletics and competition is about having fun and competing. If you are not having fun then you are missing the essence of sports. I am one of the people that you might hear say, "It's no fun if you don't win." That is true. Your fun might be moderated but I'd rather be competing and losing than be in the stands watching and cheering.

If you are blessed with the opportunity to compete, to play, to enjoy your game, understand that competing and being good at something is a temporary thing that will go away. Enjoy your sport. Enjoy your life. Make it fun and it will give you more than you possibly could even think of.

For all of the professional and college football, basketball and baseball games I have been to or participated in; for all the track meets I have been to or participated in; for all the different sporting events that I have attended, it took a run through the southern end of a park to put sports in perspective for me.

One early Sunday morning when I should have been in church, I ended up catching an early morning run in the south end of Central Park in New York City. I ran out of my hotel, crossed the street and as I trekked into the park, I ran over a bridge where I could hear a gentleman playing his saxophone. I noticed everything that was going on around me. I ran around the softball fields and saw games being played by men in khakis and collared shirts. I saw co-ed teams playing softball. I saw soccer teams practicing. I noticed all of the runners. Cyclists were everywhere, as well as roller bladers getting in their morning workout. Footballs being thrown, frisbees being thrown and baseballs being tossed, I saw just about everything on that May morning. Sports are seen as an international language because it creates a commonality in our lives. That commonality is that sports are fun.

If it's not fun for you, you need to make it fun or stop doing it. While everyone wants to win, stay in shape and/or compete, the commonality is fun. Now of course, if you are like me, you really don't have fun unless you win but that's for another section.

Sports on fun…

"I just love the game of basketball so much. The Game! I don't need the 18,000 people screaming and all the peripheral things. To me, the most enjoyable part is the practice and the preparation." - Bobby Knight

"Just play, have fun and enjoy the game." – Michael Jordan

"So many coaches forget that when they take the fun out of something, it's just not something people want to do." - Michelle Johnson

"It is impossible to excel at something you don't enjoy." - Jack Nicklaus

"Get out the wide-angle lenses, boys, I'm gettin' ready to smile!" - Fred Akers

"Remember that sports are meant to be fun. Don't let someone make the sport un-fun for you." - A.J. Kitt

"Above all, really enjoy your sport. When you are passionate about what you are doing and love doing it, you can do anything." - Carole Merle

"Athletics are like everything else. I've never seen a great athlete burn out on their sport, because they truly love what they are doing. People who get burned out on what they are doing are probably doing it for the wrong reasons." - Steve Hamilton

Acknowledgements

My Family

My wife Karen. It has been over nine years. Hopefully it doesn't feel like ninety. Your support has been unwavering, even when I did not deserve it and does not go unappreciated. Your support has allowed my confidence in this book project to rise to a level of action and your flexibility has allowed this book to finish.

Damon and Alexis, my children, my focus, my legacy: really the only thing that matters to your mother and me.

My father, the late Thomas Adams, who instilled in me a love for sports, competition, hard work, fair play and the not so lovable artistic talent of trash-talking with the best of them. Wish you could have been here to see the fruits of your labor. R.I.P.

My mother Carolyn Adams for teaching me EVERYTHING in particular sportsmanship and moderation between athletics and academics.

My brother Lamar Adams, for teaching me that it's never to late to dream and to ride out every storm and to ride it to success.

My sister, Amelia Glass, for showing me that through anything and any circumstance, success is achievable through perseverance.

My Circle of Friends

The 'March California Brotha' Traveling Conference of Encouragement. Mark Higgins, Thomas Bell, Eric Frandson and Sean Carter. Our four days together every year, no matter how much fun we have at "the tournament", have encouraged me beyond measure to drive, conquer and experience victory. Our conversations and experiences have spawned many thought processes, personal changes and many projects; even this book.

Three cheers for the purple and white... CB, we were silk and polyester when we first met, but our differences have forged a lifelong friendship. You are way too happy for me, but you are my boy. Jared Mosley (Trish, Ricky, Lisa, Nicole, Lee, Johnny) I don't even remember when, exactly, we got close but I regard you as one of my best friends and value you and your family like my own. Denise Hamilton and Tracy Ferguson. Everyone has to have "Jack and Jill" kind of friends and you two jokas are it. Mad love, to both you and your families. Dr. A. Marcus Nelson, the good doctor, continue to dream big and keep reaching. Your effect on tomorrow is enviable. Justin Frazier, through the last couple of years of undergrad and on through life, I still consider you a confidant and appreciate your candor. Jack Rich and Phil Schubert, I'll never marginalize what you two good folks taught me and allowed me to observe in action.

The Round Rock Tech Brotha's. Damon Mosley, Todd Upchurch, Jermaine McKinley, Floyd Brown and Troy Portley. The support and encouragement from the AA side of the firm was invaluable.

Ketch keep making it happen, strive for excellence and keep growing. Caren thank you so much for your support, patience and encouragement. It does or will soak in at some juncture.

Bill Whitaker, you were like a father figure to me during undergrad and your advice and ability to stand for what you believe in made me stronger. Thank you for that.

My coaches throughout high school and college... Coach Mills, Coach Scott, Coach Stephenson, Coach Fredenburg, Coach Dailey, Coach Warzbach, Coach Dyes, Coach Smith, Coach Kittley, Coach Strader and Coach Edwards. I had the opportunity to hone my skills and achieve at a high level because of the time, hard work and patience afforded to me by you good people. Thank you.

If I can inspire any athletes or fans to greater heights, deeper thoughts or a better understanding through the efforts of this book then all credit is due to God and you good people and only the mistakes have been mine.

My cup will always be half-full because of people like you.

Sean Adams
www.seanadams.net

The only non-sports based quote that will show up in this book is one of my favorite quotes ever because it speaks to attitude, imagination, dreaming and having fun.

"Know you what it is to be a child? It is to turn pumpkins into coaches, and mice into horses, lowness into loftiness and nothing into everything."

– Francis Thompson

Printed in the United States
70099LV00002BB/184-498